Mindful Lawyering

The Key to Creative Problem Solving

Kathleen Elliott Vinson
Director of Legal Writing, Research, and Written Advocacy
Professor of Legal Writing
Suffolk University Law School

Samantha Alexis Moppett
Associate Director, Legal Practice Skills Program
Professor of Legal Writing
Suffolk University Law School

Shailini Jandial George
Professor of Legal Writing
Suffolk University Law School

Carolina Academic Press
Durham, North Carolina

Library of Congress Cataloging-in-Publication Data

Names: Vinson, Kathleen Elliott, 1969-, author. | Moppett, Samantha A., author. | George, Shailini Jandial, author.
Title: Mindful lawyering : the key to creative problem solving / Kathleen Elliott Vinson, Samantha A. Moppett, and Shailini Jandial George.
Description: Durham : Carolina Academic Press, 2018. | Includes bibliographical references and index.
Identifiers: LCCN 2018004370 | ISBN 9781531002299 (alk. paper)
Subjects: LCSH: Practice of law--United States--Decision making. | Law--United States--Methodology.
Classification: LCC KF300 .V55 2018 | DDC 340/.19--dc23
LC record available at https://lccn.loc.gov/2018004370

eISBN 978-1-53100-230-5

Carolina Academic Press, LLC
700 Kent Street
Durham, North Carolina 27701
Telephone (919) 489-7486
Fax (919) 493-5668
www.cap-press.com

Printed in the United States of America

To my parents, my first teachers who inspired my love of learning and work ethic.

K.E.V.

To my mother, for her constant support, unending love, and indefatigable compassion.

S.A.M.

To my father, who has been gone for fifteen years, but whose patience, encouragement, and quiet intelligence continues to inspire me.

S.J.G.

Contents

Acknowledgments

Thank you to Suffolk University Law School for its support.

Also, we appreciate the editorial assistance of our students, including Hannah L. Sfameni, Marc Polito, Kristen Armstrong, Gustav Stickley, Erica Dumore, Courtney Fears, and Matthew Facteau. Also, thanks to David Abrams for his generosity in sharing his expertise and materials regarding problem solving.

In addition, thank you to Patti Miceli for her excellent administrative support.

Thanks to Carol McGeehan for shepherding us through the process of writing this book.

Finally, thank you to our families for their patience, encouragement, and support.

Part I

Introduction: Being a Mindful and Creative Problem Solver

What will you do when a client comes to you with a problem? Will you be ready? What approach will you take to solve it? Is knowledge of the law enough to prepare you to practice? Are you mindful? Are you creative?

Experts agree law students and lawyers need to be mindful and creative problem solvers. Many factors have coalesced to make these skills critical to the success of today's law students and lawyers such as: critiques of the traditional law school format along with curriculum changes mandated by the American Bar Association ("ABA"), the downturn in the legal market and in the changing demographics of incoming law students, and dissatisfaction among employers in their recruits' ability to solve problems independently and creatively, to name only a few.

Despite the importance of mindfulness, creativity, and problem solving to the practice of law, traditional law school courses or textbooks do not explicitly cover these topics. This book is intended to help you practice mindful lawyering, beginning in law school, to maximize your ability to creatively solve clients' problems. It discusses the skills and qualities needed to succeed in law school and in practice to successfully serve clients. It will also enhance your ability to understand and retain the legal doctrine you learn in law school.

The introduction to this book in Part I provides an overview of the scope of the book and its learning objectives and outcomes. It provides a path for your journey to becoming a mindful and creative problem solver. Part II provides the scientific basis and need for mindfulness, and encourages you to embrace your law school experience mindfully. Part III explores what it means to be a creative problem solver, why creativity is important, and how to maximize your creative potential. Part IV explains the different stages of problem solving law students and lawyers can utilize to maximize their potential for success and why lawyers need to be problem solvers. Finally, Part V synthesizes mindfulness, creativity, and problem solving, including a capstone exercise to apply the concepts learned in the book; checklists to utilize; and additional resources you can consult for more information. The book's organization into these different parts allows flexibility of use according to your needs.

Chapter One

Overview

While it may be hard to predict the future of law practice and the delivery of legal services, the need to be mindful, to think creatively, and to master the skill of problem solving, remains constant. Lawyers face numerous problems on a daily basis under stressful situations while numerous distractions compete for their attention. You may be facing a problem that you may not be able to solve within the framework of what created the problem.

So how do you handle the stress, the difficulty in focusing, and the resolution of complicated problems that may not have any easy solutions? What if you are confronted with a client who has a problem that is not the same as one in a law school casebook or hypothetical? Can you think creatively about the law to generate alternative solutions? Will a fear of failure, lack of resilience, or inability to focus on the task at hand prevent you from effective problem solving?

Transitioning from law school to practice can be challenging. Translating what you learn in the law school classroom to legal practice involves transitioning from student to legal professional. No matter what the legal issue or setting, the primary role of a lawyer is mindful and creative problem solving. Thus, to prepare you for future practice, having a solid foundation in mindful and creative problem solving is critical. Be open to new approaches to be mindful and creative in academic and legal settings and follow the steps discussed in this book to be an effective problem solver.

Below are tables setting forth three sets of learning objectives and learning outcomes for mindfulness, creativity, and problem solving. Review the tables below to see how the learning objectives are aligned with the learning outcomes. They are intended to help guide you as you make your way through this book. As you read the different parts of the book, you may find it helpful to refer back to these tables to keep focused on what you are learning, what you will be able to do after reading this book, and how it all relates to mindful lawyering as the key to creative problem solving.

A. Mindfulness Learning Objectives and Learning Outcomes

Learning Objectives **After reading this book, you will know/understand:**	**Learning Outcomes** **After reading this book, you will be able to:**
How we learn, the type of learning required in law school, and the effects of distraction and stress on that learning process.	• Understand the levels of learning. • Recognize how information is processed by the brain and the effect of distraction and stress on that process. • Reflect on your method of learning. • Appreciate the ways in which mindfulness training can help improve learning.
How to use mindfulness to train your brain to perform better.	• Realize the power of setting your intention before beginning work. • Understand how to clear your mental and physical space to allow for mindful work. • Appreciate the importance of a growth mindset. • Harness your individual grit and resiliency to spur higher levels of learning.

B. Creativity Learning Objectives and Learning Outcomes

Learning Objectives After reading this book, you will know/understand:	Learning Outcomes After reading this book, you will be able to:
What it means to be creative.	• Recognize creative ideas, products, services, and processes. • Confront the common misconceptions about creativity. • Identify the stages of the creative process. • Understand that creativity can be measured and how it is measured.
Why creativity is important.	• Appreciate the importance of creativity in light of the unprecedented rate of change today. • Recognize the role of creativity in the practice of law. • Understand the decline in creativity scores in the United States.
Strategies to maximize your creative potential.	• Reflect on the self-imposed barriers to creativity. • Embrace failure as an essential part of the creative process. • Appreciate the importance of grit and taking a break in generating novel ideas and solutions. • Recognize that there may be more than one right answer to a problem. • Understand the importance of embracing ambiguity and challenging assumptions. • Harness your creativity to generate novel solutions and ideas.

C. Problem Solving Learning Objectives and Learning Outcomes

Learning Objectives After reading this book, you will know/understand:	Learning Outcomes After reading this book, you will be able to:
How to use a systematic approach to problem solve.	• Understand the different stages of problem solving. • Identify the problem. • Develop options of how to solve the problem. • Evaluate options of how to solve the problem. • Generate and implement a plan of action to solve the problem. • Reflect on the solution.
Why lawyers need to be problem solvers.	• Understand different ways lawyers are problem solvers. • Confront uncertainties that arise when evaluating a range of possible outcomes and means of achieving those outcomes. • Apply knowledge, previous experience, and lessons learned to transfer strategies to solve different types of legal problems for different clients.

Part II

Being a Mindful Problem Solver

You sit down to read for Contracts. The professor has been cold calling, and you're feeling nervous that your turn is up soon. You really want to be well prepared and make a good impression. It's so nerve-wracking in class! You go to the library, lay out the casebook and your notebook, review the assignment, and get your laptop ready to take notes. You place your phone next to you, anticipating your roommate or your mom will be texting soon. You open your Contracts book, begin reading Hawkins v. McGee, *and start typing notes. You get through the first page, but notice that one of your friends posted some pictures from last night on social media. One is really hilarious. You share it so other friends can see. Then, back to reading. You get through another page or so, but see that friends are commenting on the picture you posted. You reply, and then go back to reading. Suddenly, you realize the Red Sox game started and decide to check the score. Wow—it's a good one! You follow along for a moment, then realize you better get back to reading. You're almost done with the case, but then your mom texts—reminding you it is your Dad's birthday. You text him, making a mental note to call him later. Back to the case again. Where were you? You don't remember if you read the last page, so you backtrack and re-read. You finish the case and begin working on a case brief, but you don't remember the details. What was the lower court decision? You re-read. What was the main issue? You re-read. What was the court's reasoning? You re-read. As you are re-reading, a feeling of dread builds in your stomach. You don't have much more time to work on this and you have a lot of other things on your mind. You start mulling over things—Dad's birthday, rent is due, dentist appointment tomorrow, Civ. Pro. homework still needs to be done, roommate wants you to go to the grocery store (what did you need again?), you are lost in Contracts.... Before you know it, your study time is over and you are not at all confident you're ready for Contracts tomorrow. Back comes the knot in your stomach, which will probably keep you from sleeping well tonight. Maybe you need to do the reading again in the morning.*

If any of this sounds familiar to you, you are not alone. Technology has drastically changed learning. The constant access to information can lead to brain overload, and paradoxically, lessen what you actually learn. This book is designed to help you harness the power of your brain and maximize your law school learning experience so that you will best be able to problem solve for your clients in the future.

By reading this book, you have already made a commitment to learn about and improve upon skills needed by law students and lawyers to better serve their clients. Perhaps you assume that your past academic success will ensure a successful law school experience as well. After all, many of us do not stop to question that which has worked well before. But law school and the practice of law are complex endeavors which are likely more challenging than what you may have experienced in the past. Why not take a step back and consider how to best approach this experience?

Chapter Two

Why Law Students Need Mindfulness Training

In the following chapters, you will learn about mindfulness and how it can help you better approach your studies, and later, your practice of law. These chapters examine how the brain processes information in order to learn and how a constant state of distraction may detract from your brain's ability to process information efficiently. You will also learn basic mindfulness techniques which can help you tackle law school and the challenges of being a lawyer in the future.

A. 21st Century Learning

It is not uncommon for new law students to struggle when adapting to the demands of law school, particularly when they are not accustomed to working in a focused, distraction-free manner. In your prior studies, you may have been able to do homework while simultaneously listening to music, periodically checking your email, responding to texts as you receive them, and constantly accessing social media. You may even have been quite successful despite this distractedness—after all, most law students are bright and have enjoyed academic success. Certainly, underachievers typically do not come to law school. But law school and law practice require a deeper focus and method of learning than you may have needed in your undergraduate studies. Upon graduating, your clients will rely on your skills and knowledge to help them with their real-life problems. Experts agree that multitasking and distractedness detract from those abilities.[1] The good news is that studying mindfully can help to combat the negative impact of multitasking and distractedness.

1. Metacognition

To understand the conflicts caused by distraction associated with multitasking, it is helpful to think about your brain and how it works. This is called "metacognition" or "awareness and understanding of one's own thought processes." Rather than going through the motions and studying the way you always have, metacognition requires that you stop and consider how you learn.

When is the last time you did this? The likely answer is never. Schooling tends to focus on what is being taught and learned, not on the process of learning itself. However, it makes sense that maximizing your learning potential will likely maximize your learning. So how do we do this?

The first step is to understand and appreciate that learning is a complex, multistep process. Bloom's Taxonomy, a framework for categorizing education goals, is helpful in understanding the levels of learning and how you can maximize yours.[2] Benjamin Bloom, with collaborators Max Englehart, Edward Furst, Walter Hill, and David Krathwohl, published a framework for categorizing educational goals which has been applied by generations of educators in teaching. The framework elaborated by Bloom and his collaborators consists of six major categories: Knowledge, Comprehension, Application, Analysis, Synthesis, and Evaluation. The categories after Knowledge were presented as "skills and abilities," with the understanding that knowledge was the necessary precondition for putting these skills and abilities into practice.[3]

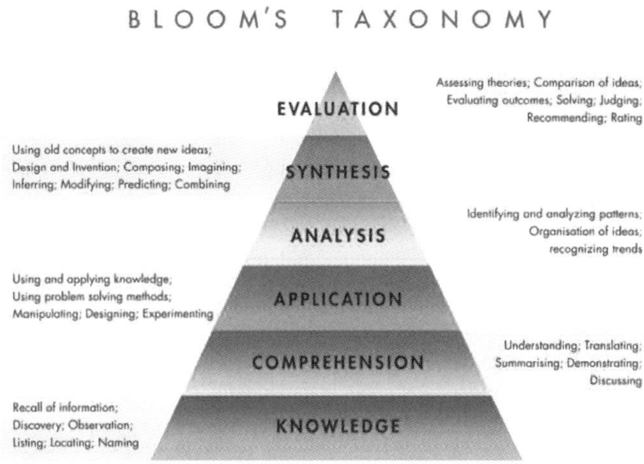

Your undergraduate studies most likely involved learning at the lower levels of the taxonomy: Knowledge, Comprehension, and Application. Knowledge, commonly thought of as learning, is at the bottom of the taxonomy. While memorization or retention of basic knowledge is a fundamental building block to achieving higher levels of learning, law school involves learning and application at the higher levels. Knowledge of the law is certainly a prerequisite to the higher levels, but alone it is not enough. Lawyers are often tasked with solving their client's problems. Clients are unique, as are their problems. That's why creativity and problem solving—which you will read about in later chapters—are so necessary. Ask any lawyer you know—they will tell you they have never faced the exact same client in the exact same situation twice. With their knowledge of the law as the foundation, lawyers must use the skills of Analysis, Synthesis, and Evaluation to apply that knowledge to each client's situation and attain the client's desired results.

Law school teaching is also conducted with an eye toward the higher levels of learning, and law practice involves the highest levels of learning. For example, law professors will often present a hypothetical situation for which you must predict the application of the law to your client's position. Professors rarely ask or test on sheer memorization of law. Similarly, in law practice, a senior attorney will rarely ask you to regurgitate black letter law. Rather, law school exams and papers, the bar exam, and problem solving on behalf of clients, require knowledge of the law in order to apply the law to new and novel situations. This necessarily requires that you have knowledge and comprehension of the law, but you must be able to apply, analyze, synthesize and evaluate the law in order to apply it to your client's situation. Law school professors may expect you to do a lot of the learning outside of the classroom and come to them with questions about what you have learned. Rarely will they use class time to focus on those lower levels of learning. They will expect that you have mastered the lower levels outside the classroom, and in turn, the knowledge required to perform at this higher level. Similarly, senior attorneys will expect that you know many of the basic law principles and that you will be able to creatively apply that law to the client's benefit to problem solve. How can you make sure you are doing this? Cognitive science can help.

2. *The Cognitive Science of Learning*

If learning at these higher levels is your goal, then it is important to know science has proven that higher-level learning involves the front part of the brain, or the frontal lobe.[4]

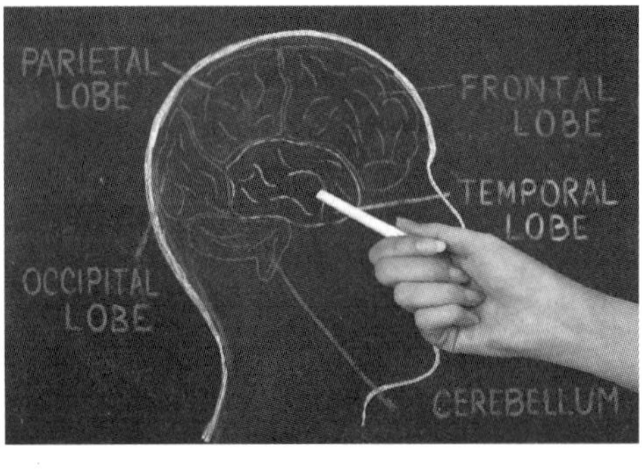

The frontal lobe houses the prefrontal cortex, the brain's manager. This is the part of the brain we use for deep focus and concentration. Many of us feel this—we rub our foreheads when engaged in deep thought or concentrated work.

The sensory part of the brain is housed in the back of the brain, or the parietal lobe.[5] This is the part of the brain that constantly scans the environment and responds to stimuli. While thousands of years ago, that scanning ensured our pre-historic ancestors' ability to respond to environmental dangers or secure the food and water needed to live, in today's world, that same part of the brain is ignited by emails, texts, and other stimuli. While this does not sound like a bad thing, it can be. Science has also proven that the more we use the part of the brain activated by distractions, such as phones and the internet, the more we weaken the part of the brain needed for deep focus.[6] In effect, the frontal lobe and parietal lobe compete, and the more you indulge distraction, the less you engage the frontal lobe. Therefore, distraction results in an inability to deeply focus.

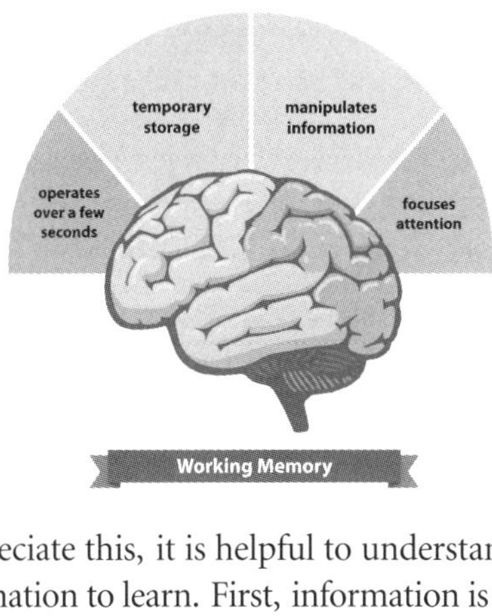

To fully appreciate this, it is helpful to understand how the brain processes information to learn. First, information is received through the parietal lobe in the back of the brain through our senses. If we pay attention to the information in some way, it makes its way through the working memory. We then must manipulate the information, such as rehearsal, or connecting it to something we already know. Eventually, information can become knowledge only when we engage the frontal cortex or the front of the brain.

Psychological Science study reveals clearing your mind can also lead to deeper thinking:

Researchers set up experiments in which people were given a collection of numbers to remember, then asked to free-associate words. Those who were asked to remember more numbers in their head had less creative replies, while those who had to remember fewer numbers gave more imaginative answers. The likely explanation: a distracted brain gets in the way of deep and agile thinking.

For our purposes, there are two primary factors that can negatively affect this learning process. The first is distraction. Because overstimulation of the parietal lobe causes weakening in the frontal lobe, the more we attend to and allow distractions, the less we will build and engage the prefrontal cortex. Think of this in terms of your smartphone: if your Wi-Fi and/or Bluetooth are constantly scanning the environment for connections, your phone's battery can get depleted. That's what distraction can do to your brain's ability to learn: it can drain the resources needed to engage in deep focus.

The second negative factor is stress. Stress activates another part of the brain, the amygdala. The hippocampus, critical to the learning process as it helps information transform from working memory into long term memory, is located near the brain's emotional center, the amygdala. Stress fires up the amygdala, which releases cortisol, which in turn interferes with hippocampus function. The more cortisol released by the amygdala, the less you are able to focus by using the prefrontal cortex.

Chronic Stress: Cortisol

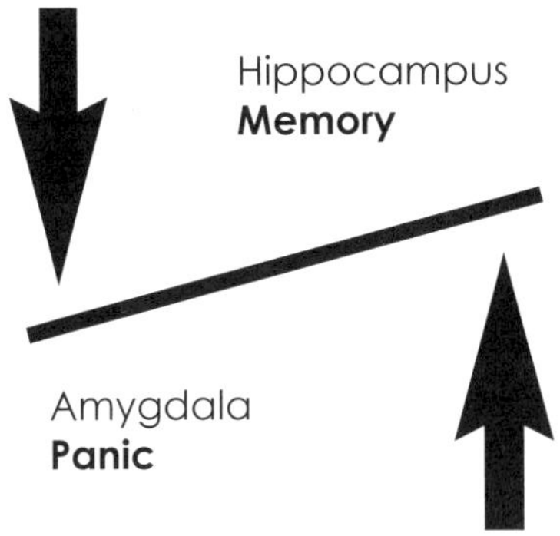

In short, stress can prevent you from learning, as increased cortisol means decreased attention, as depicted by this chart:

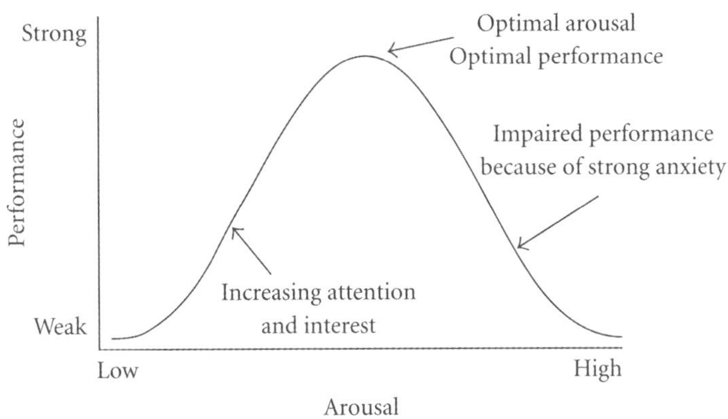

Effect of Cortisol on Attention

The good news is that mindfulness can retrain your brain and help maximize your law school experience and prepare you for law practice because it helps to strengthen the part of the brain weakened by excess distraction and to control stress so that a hyped-up amygdala cannot hijack your brain's resources.

B. The Benefits of Mindfulness

Mindfulness has received much attention, and various groups are regularly practicing mindfulness with positive results. A congressman has introduced mindfulness into weekly staff meetings on Capitol Hill; *Time* has published cover stories on mindfulness; and hospitals, corporations, professional sports teams, and even prisons have been embracing mindfulness to boost performance and productivity. In the corporate sector, mindfulness training is becoming common, partly because of successful programs at major corporations like Google. Relatively recently, secondary, undergraduate, and graduate programs have added components to their curriculums. If all of that does not convince you, consider that the American Bar Association has been promoting mindfulness since 2007.[7] Various bar associations around the country have sponsored events centered on mindfulness. If practicing lawyers are embracing the need and value of mindfulness, it makes sense that law students should too, right?

The mindfulness movement began with the Mindfulness Based Stress Reduction ("MBSR") program to help manage pain in the late 1970s.[8] While MBSR was inspired by ancient meditation practices often associated with Eastern religions, mindfulness meditation is often practiced now without any religious connotation at all. It is simply a way of focusing attention in a biological process that promotes health.

Proven success in the medical field has led to mindfulness being incorporated into other areas. It's easy to see why, when you consider that research has proven the many helpful aspects associated with its practice, such as: improving attention, working memory capacity, and academic achievement; reducing stress, anxiety, and negative emotions; and enhancing creativity, empathy, compassion, and counseling skills, and improving immunity. We hope we have now convinced you to at least consider the many benefits mindfulness can offer!

C. Mindfulness Improves Attention Which Improves Learning

Does this sum up your law school experience so far? Or, if you're just beginning, is that how you picture the experience? It does for many 1L's. Here we are talking to you about mindfulness while you are stressing over the multiple things that would rightfully trouble a 1L: grades, exams, internships, clerkships, etc. The point is—mindfulness can help you cope with all these stresses so that you can learn better, which in turn can positively impact your success in all those areas of stress.

Mindfulness has a particularly important place in learning, as it is directly connected to the very thing needed to learn: attention. Learning is a complex process. As discussed earlier, it begins with the input of information through the senses, but that information becomes knowledge only through a complex process involving different parts of the brain. The important thing for you to focus on is just that: focus. The brain can engage in this learning only when you are paying attention, and attention is weakened by distraction. Remember the Wi-Fi example: do not let that distraction drain your brain's battery. If you do, it is at the expense of your attention muscles. Essentially, the attention muscles get weak and atrophy. The back part of the brain is engaged at the cost of the front part of the brain.

How many times over the years have you been told to "pay attention"? But have you ever learned how to pay attention, or practiced paying attention? Mindfulness exercises can teach you how. Mindfulness might sound intimidating if it brings up mystical or religious connotations. It need not be—especially in the education setting. Although mindfulness is inspired by ancient practices of meditation, meditative practices such as mindfulness have taken off in many places and forms as we try to deal with the constant pressures of modern society. So, do not worry, we are not suggesting that you will begin law school by crossing your legs and chanting "OM." We know that some of you may think of meditation as a hokey waste of time. Try to set those doubts and preconceived notions aside. If you stop to think about the kind of attention you will need to absorb the intense law school experience, a mindfulness practice can help.

D. Mindfulness Training Checklist

❑ How have you typically studied in the past?

- ❍ Where?
- ❍ For how long?
- ❍ Do you sometimes become distracted? By what?

- ❑ Consider a time when you were under stress. How did it affect you physically? Mentally?
- ❑ Consider how you have dealt with stress in the past. Were you successful? What challenges have you found are created by stress?
- ❑ Can you think of a time where you handled stress well? What did you do? How did you do that?

Chapter Three

Use Mindfulness to Strengthen Your Brain

You arrive at the library, books in hand, ready to tackle your homework and empty out your backpack. The first book you see is Civ. Pro.—may as well start there! You begin reading the next cases assigned. You continue reading two cases and then remember that the professor had assigned a hypothetical to go along with one of the cases—but which one? You then pull out your notes from Civ. Pro. and see that you wrote "Don't forget hypo for class on Tuesday." You find the hypo and start drafting the answer. As you try to determine the issue, you realize you need to reread the case because you didn't know what you were supposed to be focusing on in the reading. You're about to start over when your roommate texts that she's outside and wants to chat. You go out and talk with her about her boyfriend issues. Before you realize it, 30 minutes have passed, so you go back inside and start reading the case again. It takes you two hours to get through the work even though you thought you'd have it done in the first 30 minutes at the library. Law school is so frustrating!

Hopefully you are now convinced to try mindfulness in studying. But what is mindfulness and how can you use it in your law school experience? Mindfulness is paying attention, on purpose, in the present moment, non-judgmentally. For our purposes, mindfulness simply means paying attention to what is actually taking place in the present moment instead of becoming distracted or trying to avoid reality. Being mindful allows you to focus and exercise the muscle of attention. Mindfulness is like lifting weights. Just as you can build your muscles by lifting weights, you can build your attention by practicing mindfulness.

Sounds easy, right? Try a little experiment. While you read the next paragraph, keep track of every time your thoughts jump to something else, whether it is what to have for lunch, the need to check your email, annoyance at your roommate's music, panic that you have a lot of reading due for class tomorrow, or something else. Make a little mark on a piece of paper each time some other thought creeps in while you are trying to focus on this reading. We will come back to that in a moment.

Being mindful may sound easy. But when was the last time you spent time thinking about what you are doing rather than just jumping in and doing it? When was the last time you did only one thing for an extended period of time without becoming distracted? For most of us, the answer to both questions is rarely. It probably goes something more like this: you have a homework assignment to do; you sit down, open the book, and begin doing it, without first thinking through the assignment. Why are you doing it? How does it connect to what you have already learned? What will you learn in the future? Once you are engaged in the assignment, how many times do you stop and start, checking your email, clicking back and forth between social media and your work, or just chatting with someone close by? If you are like most new law students, you probably rarely prepare yourself mentally to do the work, or focus on the work without distraction. Speaking of which, how many little marks did you make on your paper to catch your drifting thoughts while reading this paragraph? If your mind is easily distracted while reading one relatively short and simple paragraph, what will happen when the work you do is dense, complicated, and difficult to learn? This is where mindfulness can help! So, let's take it a step a time to enable you to approach your work more mindfully.

A. Set Your Intention

Our intention creates our reality.
—Wayne Dyer

> **MINDFUL WORK PROCESS**
>
> - **Set your intention**
> - Clear your physical space
> - Clear your mental space
> - Ready, set, work!

Intention is, or should be, the starting point of any action.[1] An intention is a guiding principle—an aim, a purpose, or an attitude you would like to commit to. Have you heard the phrases "What you think, you become" or "Thoughts become feelings"? Setting an intention is the first step to embodying that which you want. Acting without intention means you are acting randomly, without thought or direction. It's easy to recognize that may not be the wisest way to begin a task, and yet—be honest, how many times have you sat down to work without taking the time to consider what you are doing and why you are doing it?

Set your intention when you first sit down to engage in your assignment, before you actually begin any work. Think of this as establishing a goal for your study session, or a goal for your work session when in practice. Your intention may be to read and brief five cases, to connect the material to something you already know, to add material to your outline, to work in a distraction-free manner, or all of those and more. Try to avoid just opening a book and beginning to read. Make your goals concrete: "I will read and outline three cases, reflect on how the principles in those cases relate to what we discussed in Contracts last week, and add those principles to my outline." Do not simply have a time guideline—i.e., "I want to study for four hours." By consciously deciding what you hope to accomplish, you will have a greater chance of accomplishing it—it will not just be a happy coincidence or a failed study session. Setting your intention may take just a moment, but it is a deeply powerful tool to help you achieve your goals rather than spinning your wheels.

B. Clear Your Physical Space

MINDFUL WORK PROCESS

- Set your intention
- **Clear your physical space**
- Clear your mental space
- Ready, set, work!

Even when you know something is good for you, do you often lack the willpower to follow through with your intentions? Think of the last time you promised yourself you would not do something but did it anyway. Even if you know you should work distraction free, it is that much harder to resist the distractions if they are present and easily accessible. Removing as many distractions as possible will allow you to engage with your work at a deeper level.

Here are some simple tips to keep in mind. Although these tips are specific to studying, the principals apply equally to practice, when you will have multiple clients, assignments, and issues competing for your attention.

First, choose a physical space that is conducive to your work. For example, if you are writing a legal memorandum, you may need to consult many different sources—cases, statutes, and notes, all at the same time. You must have hardcopies of the materials; you cannot do your best work while toggling between documents on your laptop or computer. It is simply too much for your brain to switch back and forth. Make sure you are working in an area that allows you to spread these materials out. Whereas if you are reading for Torts, for example, you may only need the textbook, a notebook, and your laptop or computer. Have only the materials you need for your assignment on the table, this will allow you to focus on the material at hand.

Second, if you are using your computer and cannot turn off your Internet access, consider disconnecting any automatic alerts you may have so that you do not get pop up alerts of new emails, social media postings, sports scores, etc. Each time one of these alerts goes off, your brain desperately wants to be distracted and attend to them. Do not allow that to happen. One recent study found that it can take your brain 15–25 minutes to get back to where it was after stopping to check an email. You do not want to waste that much time every time you check an email, do you? It will be hard at first, but set a time limit to work and a time for breaks. Fifty-five minutes is a reasonable amount of time to focus on a task before taking a break. At that point, your brain probably needs a break and you can check your email. But only take a 5-minute break to refresh yourself and then get back to work. Any longer and you begin to forget where you were.

Third, put your smartphone away. Unless you are expecting an emergency call, there is rarely a time you cannot be without it for a minimum of 55 minutes. We've become used to instant feedback and responses, but know that each time you start and stop working, you are actually leaking a little mental efficiency. In fact, one study showed that pot smokers were more efficient than multitaskers.[2] Knowing that should motivate you not to multitask!

With your physical and mental spaces clear and ready to work, your brain can best attend to and focus on the material at hand.

C. Clear Your Mental Space

Once you have established what you want to accomplish in your study session, it is time to clear your mind to enable you to accomplish it. This can be done in many ways, but mindfully breathing for a few minutes is an easy and simple way to begin. Use your breath to help settle your mind and body to enable you to work most productively. Studies

> **MINDFUL WORK PROCESS**
> - Set your intention
> - Clear your physical space
> - **Clear your mental space**
> - Ready, set, work!

have shown that slow, deep breathing activates areas of the brain which counteract depression, helps insomniacs wake up fewer times at night, and significantly reduces anxiety.

Here is one breathing exercise you can try that walks through the process very specifically, which is helpful when first trying to control and harness your breath:

- *Begin by sitting up straight and putting your feet flat on the floor.*
- *Your hands should be on your lap or down by your side, whichever is more comfortable.*
- *Close your eyes or focus on one spot in the room.*
- *Roll your shoulders slowly forward and then slowly back.*
- *Lean your head from side to side; try to relax your muscles.*
- *Observe your breathing. Notice how your breath flows in and out.*
- *Make no effort to change your breathing in any way, simply notice how your body breathes. Your body knows how much air it needs.*
- *Sit quietly, seeing in your mind's eye your breath flowing gently in and out of your body. When your attention wanders, as it will, just focus back again on your breathing.*
- *Notice any stray thoughts, but don't dwell on them. Simply let the thoughts pass.*
- *See how your breath continues to flow … deeply … calmly.*
- *Notice the stages of a complete breath … from the in breath … to the pause that follows … the exhale … and the pause before taking another breath.…*
- *Feel the air entering through your nose … picture the breath flowing through the cavities in your sinuses and then down to your lungs.…*
- *As thoughts intrude, allow them to pass, and return your attention to your breathing.*
- *Feel your chest and stomach gently rise and fall with each breath.*
- *Now as you inhale, count silently … one.*
- *As you exhale, count … one.*
- *Wait for the next breath, and count again … one.*

- *Exhale … one.*
- *Inhale … one.*
- *Exhale … one.*
- *Continue to count each inhalation and exhalation as "one."*
- *Notice now how your body feels.*
- *See how calm and gentle your breathing is, and how relaxed your body feels.*
- *Now it is time to gently reawaken your body and mind.*
- *Open your eyes, and remain sitting for a moment longer.*
- *Straighten out your legs, and stretch your arms and legs gently.*[3]

While you are breathing mindfully, if thoughts keep popping into your head, jot them down. Maybe you need to remember to make a phone call, send an email, or follow up on some other matter. If those thoughts keep creeping in, you must attend to them. But not now. Set those notes aside, knowing you will attend to them after you complete the work you have intended to do. Now you know you will not forget and your brain can relax into the work you intended to complete.

This is just one guided breathing exercise, there are multiple exercises you can try; the Internet is literally full of them. Download a guided meditation to your smartphone and you can use it wherever you are—the library, your room, a busy airport—whenever or wherever you need to quiet your mind. Let your smartphone be more than just a distraction!

In addition to breathing, there are other ways to help clear your mental space. For some, a quick burst of exercise can help clear the mind to prepare for work. Consider it giving your brain a break and resetting. A quick walk outside, jumping jacks, running in place, or doing pushups for a minute will all get your blood pumping and help flush out thoughts which may have been lingering that could potentially interfere with the work you have planned.[4]

Here is a less structured breathing exercise that you can use anytime you are feeling stressed. Try 4-7-8 breathing—a "natural tranquilizer for the nervous system."

- *Exhale completely through your mouth, making a whoosh sound.*
- *Close your mouth and inhale quietly through your nose to a mental count of **four**.*
- *Hold your breath for a count of **seven**.*
- *Exhale completely through your mouth, making a whoosh sound to a count of **eight**.*
- *This is one breath. Now inhale again and repeat the cycle three more times for a total of four breaths.*

Note that you always inhale quietly through your nose and exhale audibly through your mouth. The tip of your tongue stays in position the whole time. Exhalation takes twice as long as inhalation. The absolute time you spend on each phase is not important; the ratio of 4:7:8 is important. If you have trouble holding your breath, speed the exercise up but keep to the ratio of 4:7:8 for the three phases. With practice you can slow it all down and get used to inhaling and exhaling more and more deeply.

This exercise is a natural tranquilizer for the nervous system.

Once you develop this technique by practicing it every day, it will be a very useful tool that you will always have with you. Use it whenever anything upsetting happens—before you react. Use it whenever you are aware of internal tension. Use it to help you fall asleep. This exercise cannot be recommended too highly. Everyone can benefit from it.

D. Ready, Set, Work!

Now that you have set your intention and cleared your mental and physical space, you are truly ready to work. One of tenets of

MINDFUL WORK PROCESS

- Set your intention
- Clear your physical space
- Clear your mental space
- **Ready, set, work!**

mindfulness is that while staying in the moment, you should try not to be judgmental about the thoughts that may creep in. For example, while you are studying for an exam, you may find yourself thinking about the grade you received on the last exam or assignment in that class. Suppose you were unhappy with that grade. Your mind may keep turning to that, mulling it over while you are trying to focus on your upcoming exam. Thinking to yourself "I'm not as smart as my classmates who did better than me," or "I'll never get an A" are self-destructive, self-fulfilling thoughts. The reverse is also a problem—the "I did well last time so I'll probably do well this time," thought process can also derail your mind as it prevents you from fully engaging in the work at hand. Mindfulness means letting go of those thoughts to allow you to stay in the moment and refocus your intention for that session. Remember to fall back on techniques we talked about earlier in this chapter. Jot down thoughts which intrude, try not to judge yourself, and refocus your attention on the work at hand. In addition to those basic mindfulness techniques, here are a few more things to consider.

1. Grit

You may have heard the term "grit," as educators are embracing grit as a key element needed for academic success. Grit is defined as a characteristic that captures people's ability to persevere in the face of difficulty. Grit is highly predictive of students' willingness to put forth the effort needed to learn.[5] Psychologist Angela Duckworth presents this equation to describe the psychology of achievement:

Skill x Effort = Achievement

Talent x Effort = Skill

Therefore:

(Talent x Effort) x Effort = Achievement[6]

While some may focus a lot on the talent part of the equation—that idea that we are born with a certain amount of intelligence that dictates our potential for academic achievement, the equation places twice as much weight on effort! That's why grit, the willingness to put forth that effort, is so important.

If effort is that important, it's worth considering, what do we mean by effort? One term for the kind of effort needed to learn is deliberate practice: setting a specific goal, fully concentrating on a single task, receiving immediate and informative feedback, and practicing repetitively until fluent. Because of the repetition and difficulty of the work, deliberate practice is quite effortful and you may not find it "fun," but it is effective. Thankfully, grit is malleable: your grit can, and ideally should, change over time.

How gritty are you? Here's a test you can take to assess.[7] Following are a number of statements that may or may not apply to you. There are no right or wrong answers, so just answer honestly, considering how you compare to most people. At the end, you'll get a score that reflects how passionate and persevering you see yourself to be.

1. New ideas and projects sometimes distract me from previous ones.
    - Very much like me
    - Mostly like me
    - Somewhat like me
    - Not much like me
    - Not like me at all
2. Setbacks don't discourage me. I don't give up easily.
    - Very much like me
    - Mostly like me
    - Somewhat like me

- Not much like me
- Not like me at all

3. I often set a goal but later choose to pursue a different one.
   - Very much like me
   - Mostly like me
   - Somewhat like me
   - Not much like me
   - Not like me at all
4. I am a hard worker.
   - Very much like me
   - Mostly like me
   - Somewhat like me
   - Not much like me
   - Not like me at all
5. I have difficulty maintaining my focus on projects that take more than a few months to complete.
   - Very much like me
   - Mostly like me
   - Somewhat like me
   - Not much like me
   - Not like me at all
6. I finish whatever I begin.
   - Very much like me
   - Mostly like me
   - Somewhat like me
   - Not much like me
   - Not like me at all
7. My interests change from year to year.
   - Very much like me
   - Mostly like me
   - Somewhat like me

- Not much like me
- Not like me at all

8. I am diligent. I never give up.
   - Very much like me
   - Mostly like me
   - Somewhat like me
   - Not much like me
   - Not like me at all
9. I have been obsessed with a certain idea or project for a short time but later lost interest.
   - Very much like me
   - Mostly like me
   - Somewhat like me
   - Not much like me
   - Not like me at all
10. I have overcome setbacks to conquer an important challenge.
    - Very much like me
    - Mostly like me
    - Somewhat like me
    - Not much like me
    - Not like me at all

Scoring:

For odd numbered questions (1, 3, 5, 7, 9) assign the following points: 1 = very much like me, 2 = mostly like me, 3 = somewhat like me, 4 = not much like me, 5 = not like me at all.

For even numbered questions (2, 4, 6, 8, 10) assign the following points: 5 = very much like me, 4 = mostly like me, 3 = somewhat like me, 2 = not much like me, 1 = not like me at all.

Next, add up all the points and divide by 10. The maximum score on this scale is 5 (extremely gritty) and lowest on this scale is 1 (not at all gritty).

If you discovered you are very gritty, congratulations! If you discovered you could be grittier, mindfulness can help. First, through keeping your thoughts focused on tasks in front of you and controlling your "grass is always greener" thinking (I could be doing something else, others do not have to study as much as I do, etc.), you will increase your effort and grit.

The second major way to increase grit is through promoting a growth mindset. The theory of "growth mindset," pioneered by Carol Dweck, is based on the theory that individuals' thinking is dominated by either a growth or a fixed mindset when learning something new.[8] Educational psychologists determined that a growth mindset allows for greater success in advancing the academic agenda. What is a growth mindset? A growth mindset means believing that intelligence can be developed through effort. Having a growth mindset leads to a desire to learn and a tendency to embrace challenges, persist in the face of setbacks, see effort as a path to mastery, learn from criticism, and find lessons and inspiration in the success of others. All this gives people with a growth mindset a greater sense of free will, and allows for improvement through positive feedback loops. Those with a growth mindset are grittier.

Those who believe intelligence is static and that achievement potential is predetermined are said to have a "fixed" mindset. Those with a fixed mindset avoid challenges because of a fear of failure; they may give up easily, see effort as fruitless, ignore useful negative feedback, and feel threatened by the success of others. The end result of this fixed mindset is that you may plateau early and achieve less than your full potential. Those with a fixed mindset also tend to lack grit.

You likely experienced academic success before entering law school. Maybe you also performed well on the LSAT. You may have been told that you were smart and believe that this given intelligence will allow you to conquer law school easily. This is a fixed mindset approach, and may not allow you to embrace learning. While most of us have some of both mindsets, approaching law school with an open mind and a growth mindset will allow you to learn and adapt to this new environment, to take in the feedback and challenges, and to embrace your new skills. A growth mindset is essential to the process of metacognition and mindfulness, and therefore, academic success. Cultivating these characteristics now will allow you to approach the challenging practice of law with the greatest chance of success as well.

2. Repeat A, B, and C as Necessary

We have now covered the essential skills needed to work more mindfully. Suppose you commit yourself to these steps, follow each, and understand the need for grit and a growth mindset, but you receive a low grade on an exam or paper, or an issue with a client in your law practice results in an unfavorable outcome. Does that mean our system has failed you? Of course not! That is the time to refocus and commit yourself even further to approaching your work mindfully. You may find that you easily question yourself, your capability, your decision to attend to law school, or your choice of jobs. While these concerns are natural and real, they are not about what you are doing at the moment are they? This is the kind of judgmental thinking you should seek to avoid by engaging in a mindfulness approach. So, go back to Steps A, B, and C—set your intention, clear your mental space, clear your physical space (you're not staring at that paper, are you?), and get back to work!

E. Train Your Brain Checklist

Reflect on a recent study or work session. What was your intention before you began? Were you distracted? Was your physical space conducive to the work you were trying to accomplish? Once you have tried the techniques described in this chapter, use this checklist to evaluate your work:

- ❑ Did you create a plan before you began?
- ❑ Did you clear your physical space to make it conducive and specific to the work at hand?

- ❏ Did you clear your mental space to help eliminate distractions and create a focused learning environment?
- ❏ Did you note items distracting you so that you could attend to them later?
- ❏ Did you try to work with grit and resiliency, reminding yourself not to dwell on past mistakes or failures?

Part III

Being a Creative Problem Solver

You are celebrating your six-month anniversary at your first job after law school. You sit down for lunch at your desk and decide to check your social media accounts. You post a picture of yourself sitting at your desk—#crushingit, #livingthedream, #thisiswhatlawyersdo. The first six months went well and the attorneys who you work with seem nice. You also love Boston and are looking forward to your first St. Patrick's Day as a Boston resident. As your phone rings, you hear the familiar "ping" alerting you to a new email in your inbox. You click to open and see it's from your friend, Cheyenne, who you saw at a party on Saturday night. She reminds you of a conversation you had at the party about her older sister, Alameda, who lives in Connecticut. Alameda received a letter saying that Ryer's department store is planning to sue her for a violation of a non-compete if she doesn't quit her job as a personal stylist at the high-end department store, Brandhorst's. Cheyenne asks for your help—she tells you that Alameda loves working at Brandhorst's and doesn't want to leave. You take a look at the letter that Cheyenne has sent as an attachment to the email.

You think to yourself, what luck! It would be great to bring some work to the firm and this issue is right up your alley. You vaguely remember one of the problems you had in your Employment Law class was a noncompete issue—except in a different jurisdiction. After some searching you locate the memorandum of law that you wrote in support of a motion to dismiss. You received an A on the assignment and decide to adapt the memo to the current case.

As you are working on the memo, your supervising attorney drops by your office and asks you what you are working on. Excitedly, you tell her about the case and what you are doing. When you are done, your supervising attorney is quiet. She then suggests that you may not want to spend any more billable hours on the memo without first thinking about more creative solutions to Cheyenne's problem.

You start to freak out. You think to yourself, I'm not creative. And, what does creativity have to do with the practice of law? Artists need to be creative, not lawyers. Lawyers need to research and apply the law. What does she mean? How can you be creative? What am I going to do?

As you learned earlier, mindfulness enhances your creativity. Mindfulness forces you to think on how to think. By quieting your mind and focusing your attention, you permit your creative genius to flow. But, you may be wondering, what does creativity have to do with being a lawyer?

As you have already read, lawyers are essentially problem solvers. As a lawyer, you will have different types of clients with many types of problems. Reading redacted cases in casebooks throughout law school may lead you to believe that there is one resolution to a problem. In fact, this couldn't be further from the truth. The resolution to a problem depends on the specific facts and the client's particular needs and desires. One size does not fit all. There is no machine where facts and law are entered and THE answer pops out.

This is where creativity comes in. In a nutshell, being creative allows a lawyer to see a problem from various viewpoints and develop multiple solutions to the problem, thus enhancing problem-solving practices. The first chapter in this part of the book will provide an introduction to creativity. The next chapter addresses why it is important to be creative. Finally, the last chapter in this part will set forth some ways that you can work to maximize your creative potential.

Chapter Four

Creativity 101

Creativity has long been considered a somewhat mysterious concept that defies definition. Frequently, it is referred to as one of those things that "you'll know it when you see it." While creative people, products, and processes have been around and recognized for centuries, the study of creativity is relatively new. In fact, the study of the science of creativity began in earnest in 1950.

A. Definition of Creativity

Creativity is seeing what everyone else has seen, and thinking what no one else has thought.
—Albert Einstein

These words—creative and creativity—are probably words that you have been hearing a lot lately. While they may be some of today's buzzwords, what is creativity? What does it mean to be creative?

Creative Idea = Novel + Useful

Currently, there are over 100 definitions of creativity. That being said, scholars generally agree that creative thought or behavior has two parts. First, an idea or work is creative if it is novel. Here, novel means original or unexpected. Novelty alone, however, is not sufficient because, as you have probably experi-

Shoe umbrellas: Mini-umbrellas that attach to the toes of your shows to protect them from the rain. Novel, yes! Socially valuable?

enced, an idea or work that is novel can be completely ridiculous. Second, for a thought or behavior to be considered creative, it must also be useful or socially valuable. Accordingly, creative people are able to solve problems by developing original ideas that are useful.

By this definition, to be considered creative, an idea, product, service, or process need not be unprecedented. Rather, it need only improve on existing knowledge. Arthur Koestler, in his 1964 book, *The Act of Creation*, poignantly recognized this when he wrote:

> The creative act is not an act of creation in the sense of the Old Testament. It does not create something out of nothing: it uncovers, selects, re-shuffles, combines, synthesizes already existing facts, ideas, faculties, skills. The more familiar the parts, the more striking the new whole.[1]

Take the iPhone, for example. Although not a completely new concept, Steve Jobs, the CEO of Apple, was creative when he came up with the idea. Jobs combined preexisting ideas—the iPod, a camera, a GPS, the iTunes store, a cell phone, and an Internet browser—to create a new product.

Note that people are not creative in the abstract. Knowledge is fundamental to creative thinking. Therefore, when people are creative, they are creative in a particular domain. As discussed more fully below, the domains within which a person can be creative are vast. A person can be creative in writing, business, marketing, engineering, etc.

Another current buzzword related to creativity is innovation. Creativity is an essential building block of innovation. While creativity refers to the ability to generate novel and useful ideas, innovation is the process of implementing a creative idea into a marketable product or service. Innovation entails turning creative ideas into reality.

Innovation =
Creative Idea + Implementation

For example, Sara Blakely was innovative when she invented Spanx. Working in Florida selling fax machines door-to-door, Sara was required to wear pantyhose in the hot and humid climate. While she liked that the control-top of the pantyhose eliminated panty lines, she hated the look of the seamed foot in her sandals. To solve the problem, Sara generated a novel and useful idea when she cut the feet off of her pantyhose.

This is where innovation comes in—turning a creative idea into reality. Once she had the idea, she spent two years and $5000 in savings to develop her idea. Unable to locate a female patent attorney in Georgia, she purchased a book and wrote her own patent application. When she called hosiery mills in North Carolina, they all rejected her idea. Two weeks after leaving North Carolina, a mill operator with three daughters that loved Sara's idea called Sara and offered to support her concept. She created a prototype, decided on a brand name, and marketed the product to department stores. She convinced Neiman Marcus to carry the product, and multiple retailers followed. Around this time, Sara sent a box of her products to Oprah Winfrey and, in 2000, Oprah named Spanx her favorite product of the year. The rest is history. Spanx, footless pantyhose, and an entirely new category in women's retail—shapewear—was born.

B. Creativity Myths

Before you go any further, it may be helpful to address some of the common misconceptions about creativity, many of which have probably run through your head since you began to read this chapter. While there is no truth to them, most people still believe these myths. The first step is to dispel any of these myths. These limiting beliefs can act as barriers to maximizing your creative potential.

1. The Smarter You Are, the More Creative You Are

Contrary to popular belief, creativity and intelligence are not the same thing. Intelligence is defined as a person's ability to attain and apply knowledge and skills. The term intelligence also tends to be associated with academic ability. As you are undoubtedly aware, these cognitive abilities are measured by an Intelligence Quotient—or IQ—test.

Researchers have discovered that in order to be creative, a person must have an IQ of approximately 120. An IQ above this score, however, does not equate to higher creativity. Intelligence and creativity are statistically independent: highly creative people may or may not be highly intelligent individuals.

So, don't worry—you don't need to be Einstein to be creative!

2. Creativity is Confined to the Arts

People tend to equate the word creative with artistic. As such, creativity is most often associated with activities like the arts, advertising, design, and marketing. People and organizations, however, can be creative whenever they use their intelligence. Creativity can be expressed in a wide range of areas including science, mathematics, teaching, medicine, coaching, engineering, and yes, even the law. You can address almost any task—washing the car, playing a game of tennis, or work—in a creative manner.

3. Creativity is Limited to the Rare Few—Either You Have It or You Don't

To my mind it is a mistake to think of creative activity as something unusual.
—Jacob Bronowski, author of *The Ascent of Man*

Another common misperception is that creativity is limited to a rare few special people. Face it, how many times have you said—or heard someone else say—"I'm not creative." Creativity tends to be considered a fixed trait—like being able to roll your tongue or touch the tip of your nose with your tongue. Either you have it or you don't. Feeding into this misconception is the fact that creativity tends to be associated with creative geniuses like Emily Dickinson, Sigmund Freud, Steve Jobs, William Shakespeare, and Pablo Picasso.

Geniuses, however, do not have a monopoly on creativity. Rather, creativity is a regular part of everyone's thinking and behavior. Everyone is born with creative abilities, but at different levels. The challenge is to cultivate your creative capacities.

Recognizing that everyone has creative potential, researchers have categorized creativity via creative magnitude, differentiating between Big-C and little-c creativity.

a. Big-C Creativity

The unmistakable examples of creative expression of the creative geniuses listed above are examples of Big-C creativity. Dickinson's poems, Freud's psychology, Jobs' revolutionary technologies, Shakespeare's plays, and Picasso's paintings are all instances of remarkable achievements that transformed and altered a field of study in a profound way. Big-C creativity encompasses the relatively rare demonstrations of creativity that have a large impact on others and the world.

Can you think of other examples of Big-C creativity?

- Louis Armstrong's music
- Marie Curie's theory of radioactivity
- Charles Darwin's theory of evolution
- Jack Dorsey's microblog, Twitter
- T.S. Eliot's verse
- Lady Gaga's unconventional and provocative singing, song writing, and acting
- Mahatma Ghandi's leadership
- Mark Zuckerberg's social networking website, Facebook

b. Little-c Creativity

On the other hand, little-c creativity refers to everyday creativity. Everyday creativity refers to an individual's ability to solve problems that arise on a daily basis and to readily adapt to change. Unlike the earth-shattering contributions of the creative geniuses that demonstrate Big-C creativity, little-c creativity results in useful and significant contributions to day-to-day life.

If you stop to think about it, ordinary people come up with good ideas all the time. Examples of little-c creativity include coming up with different ways to fix lawn mowers, dishwashers, and refrigerators; creating a dinner from the leftovers in the refrigerator; making wallets out of duct tape; teaching a dog new tricks; improving a process; or creating a new football play.

A "lifehack" is another example of little-c creativity. Lifehacks are techniques that allow you to do or manage a day-to-day activity more efficiently. Numerous websites exist that provide countless examples of creative ways to simplify tasks in everyday life.

Using a fork to keep a taco from falling over

Creating an iPhone speaker with tacks and a toilet paper roll

Preventing a popsicle from dripping with a cupcake liner

4. Creativity Can't Be Controlled

> *Inspiration is for amateurs. The rest of us just show up and get to work.*
> —Chuck Close, artist

A fourth misconception about creativity is that it can't be controlled. Rather, ideas just come to you in the "Aha" or "Eureka" moment. Accordingly, you have to simply wait for inspiration to strike.

This couldn't be further from the truth. The Eureka moment—when an idea suddenly appears—is simply the result of hard work. In fact, it represents the third stage of the creative process.

FOUR STAGES OF THE CREATIVE PROCESS

- Preparation
- Incubation
- Illumination
- Verification

The first stage, Preparation, involves identifying and defining the issue to be addressed and collecting information necessary to solve the problem. As discussed later in the book, when solving a problem, this involves identifying the client, determining the facts, ascertaining the client's objectives, understanding the relevant law and how it could apply, recognizing the ethical and moral issues, considering alternative solutions, and collaborating with others. It also involves conducting the necessary research to attain the requisite domain knowledge. For the next stage, the problem is then set aside.

After much hard work, creative ideas tend to percolate when the mind is distracted during the second stage of the creative process—Incubation. During this second stage, the creator takes a break from the problem. With the mind left free to wander, creative ideas arise as the brain makes connections that it wouldn't otherwise.

It is only after all this work that the Eureka moment occurs in the third stage, Illumination. During this stage, the creator suddenly realizes the solution to the problem. This is why you frequently hear people saying that they get their best ideas while showering, gardening, or running on the treadmill.

The final stage is Verification. During this stage, the creator evaluates whether the idea is a good one and then uses critical thinking skills to fashion the idea into a finished product.

5. Creativity Can't be Taught

Inevitably, a thought that comes to mind is, "OK, so while everyone is creative, I'm not very creative and it's not something that I can improve."

On the contrary, researchers have discovered that it is possible to foster your creativity. While it is not possible to increase your inborn potential, it is possible to work to maximize your creative potential. Think of creativity as a muscle that everyone is born with. Like any muscle, the ability to be creative increases and strengthens with practice. A future chapter will address some ways to flex your creative muscle.

6. Creativity Occurs in Isolation

This last myth that creativity occurs when a lone genius slaves away in isolation is one of the most prevalent misconceptions about creativity. Pictures of Steve Jobs in the early days of Apple, a company that he helped to start, epitomize the myth of the lone genius. Frequently, he is pictured alone in a room with a dearth of furniture and decor. This is what many people envision when they think of the creative process.

In fact, creativity is a collaborative process. The work and ideas of other people kindle an individual's creativity. Despite the archetypal image of Steve Jobs as a lone genius working long, lonely hours to create the iPod and iPhone, Jobs collaborated fanatically. When pioneering both the iPod and the iPhone, Jobs collaborated with multiple people at Apple, particularly Jonathan Ives—the chief designer at Apple. According to Jobs, "innovation comes from people meeting in the hallways or calling each other … [I]t's *ad hoc* meetings of six people called by someone who thinks he has figured out the coolest new thing ever and wants to know what other people think of his idea."[2] Benefits of collaboration, specifically in the context of the problem-solving process, are discussed later in the book.

C. Measuring Creativity

Contrary to the popular belief that creativity is far too complex to be measured, there is a long history of creativity tests. Tests exist to measure creativity, ascertain how the individual is creative, and identify the creative strengths and weaknesses of an individual. The most prominent evaluation methods concentrate on the creative process and creative thinking, measuring the cognitive abilities indicative of creativity. The objective is to be able to predict which individuals will generate a creative product.

The Torrance Test of Creative Thinking ("TTCT") is the most well-known test employed to gauge a person's creative aptitude. The TTCT is built upon the work of J.P. Guilford, who identified two distinct types of thinking—convergent and divergent. Convergent thinking refers to coming up with the "one-right-answer." Convergent thinking can be effective in circumstances where an answer exists or can be figured out from what is previously known through the use of conventional search, identification, and decision-making strategies. It is also helpful in the Verification stage of the creative process. It is not, however, conducive to the production of novel solutions to problems.

In contrast, divergent thinking involves mental processes that allow a person to generate multiple possible solutions to open-ended questions or problems. This ability to explore multiple alternative responses is conducive to the formation of new and original ideas. It is also important to defer judgment on the ideas generated, as this can negatively impact the generation of novel ideas. Divergent thinking is critical to creativity and creative problem solving.

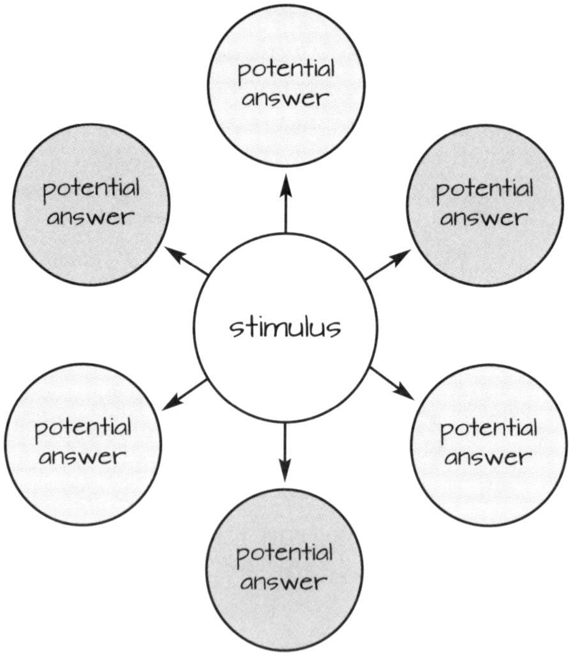

Not surprisingly, the tests used to assess creativity generally involve measuring divergent thinking. Building on Guilford's work, psychologist E. Paul Torrance developed the TTCT which requires test takers to provide multiple responses to both Figural and Verbal

Tests. The Figural Tests entail thinking creatively with pictures while the Verbal Tests entail thinking creatively with words. Each test measures different creative thinking abilities.

To assist in evaluating an individual's creativity, divergent thinking has been operationalized into four components:

1. Originality: The unusualness of the responses relative to the responses of others within the specific group of test takers.
2. Fluency: The total number of relevant responses generated.
3. Flexibility: The number of diverse categories of relevant responses.
4. Elaboration: The level of detail in the responses.

To understand how these components are used to evaluate creativity, let's take a look at one of the Figural Tests in the TTCT that entails thinking creatively with pictures. In this test, test takers are asked to create as many drawings as they can out of a shape that is provided. If five people were asked to take a few minutes to draw as many different things as they could with a circle as a starting point, the following responses could be evaluated as follows:

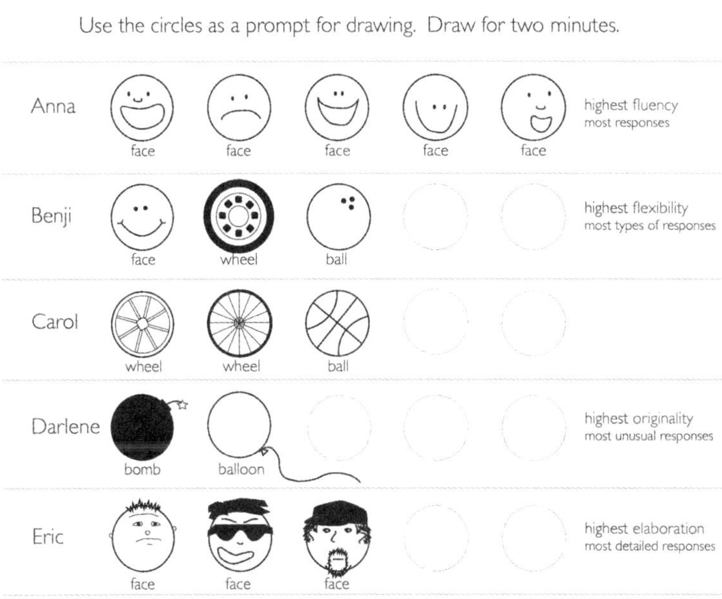

- Anna has the highest *fluency* because, although all of the drawings are of faces, she drew the most drawings.
- Benji has fewer responses than Anna, but has the highest *flexibility* because he provided the largest number of types of responses.
- Carol does not prevail on any of the components.
- Darlene has the highest *originality* because, although only providing two responses, none of the other responses included a balloon or a bomb.
- Finally, Eric has the highest *elaboration* because, although he only drew three faces, the faces have more detail than the others.[3]

Another Figural Test asks test takers to use a shape provided to draw a picture, combine shapes that are provided to create a picture, or to complete a picture using the incomplete figures provided. An example of each of the three tasks in the Figural Test appear below.

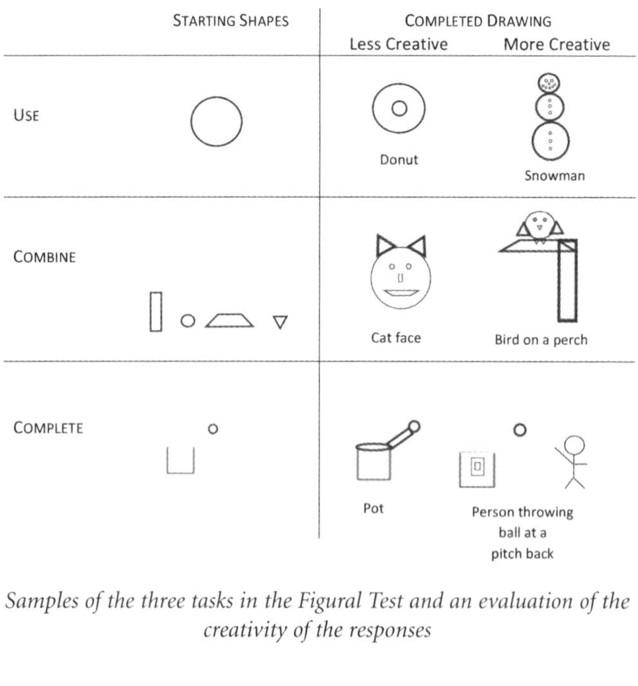

Samples of the three tasks in the Figural Test and an evaluation of the creativity of the responses

In contrast, the Verbal Test entails thinking creatively with words. One task in the Verbal Test asks test takers to come up with alternative uses for an everyday object. For example, the test may ask the test taker to list as many possible uses for an everyday object such as a brick, cup, or paperclip. A sample brainstorm of uses for a paperclip could include:

- holding papers together
- cufflinks
- earrings
- imitation mini-trombone
- keeping headphones from getting tangled up
- bookmark[4]

If you think about it, this is similar to the lifehacks discussed previously.

Now you know what it means to be creative and that creativity can be measured. More importantly, you are now aware of the myths that prevail around the concept of creativity. You don't need to be a Nobel Prize winner to be creative. Everyone is creative and creativity is an integral part of life.

The next chapter will address the "So what?" question that you may find yourself asking. Specifically, it will address why creativity is important and why you should work to maximize your creative potential.

D. Creativity 101 Checklist

❑ Consider the creativity myths that you read about.

  ❍ Before you read about them, did you believe any of them?

    - Did you believe that smarter people are more creative?
    - Did you believe that creativity only applies to the arts?

    - Did you believe that creativity is limited to only a rare few special people?
    - Did you believe that creativity can't be controlled and that you just need to sit around and wait for inspiration to strike?
    - Did you believe that creativity can't be fostered or taught?
    - Did you believe that people are creative in isolation and that creativity is not a collaborative process?
  - ❍ If so, have you been able to dispel the myth(s) so that it (they) can no longer serve as a barrier to your creative potential?
- ❑ Are you surprised that creativity can be measured? Why or why not?
- ❑ Do you consider yourself a convergent thinker or a divergent thinker? Both? Explain.
- ❑ Measure your creativity—
  - ❍ In three minutes, draw as many drawings as you can out of the rectangles below. After three minutes, review your responses. Are they original, fluent, flexible, and elaborate?

  - ❍ Now, take three minutes and list as many possible uses of a brick as you can. How did you do?
- ❑ Can you think of an example of a creative idea that you came up with to solve an everyday problem?

Chapter Five

Creativity: Why It's Needed Now More Than Ever

Now that you know what creativity is and the common myths surrounding creativity, you may find yourself asking, "Who cares?" Is creativity even important? This chapter will discuss why creativity is an indispensable trait in today's fast-changing climate. Lawyers need to be creative in order to fulfill their obligations to clients. Contrary to prevailing stereotypes, lawyers do more than mechanically apply the rule of law. To succeed, lawyers need to cultivate their creative capacities so they can generate novel solutions to problems.

A. Unprecedented Rate of Change

[Creativity] is no longer a luxury for a few,
but ... a necessity for all.
—Mihaley Csikszentmihalyi, cofounder of positive psychology

The world is now changing at mind-bending speed, and this pace of change is only likely to quicken. The technological revolution exemplifies this unprecedented rate of change. Consider the changes in technology over the last 50 years. Fifty years ago, cable didn't exist. Televisions had only six stations and you had to get up to change the channel. There was no such thing as a VHS or a DVD player to allow you to rent and watch movies at home, let alone Netflix. Forget cell phones—cordless phones didn't even exist. Push button phones rather than rotary dial phones were a luxury.

Next, consider the Internet. This term was first used in 1974. In 1992, there were over one million Internet hosts. Five years later, this number rose to 20 million, and in January 2016, it was reported that there were approximately 1.05 billion Internet hosts. Moving from Internet hosts to Internet users, by 2010, it was reported that there were almost two billion users of the Internet worldwide. Fast forward to March 2017—the number of Internet users increased to 3.74 billion, representing more than 40% of the world population. Moreover, in 2017, the Internet traffic was greater than the compilation of all earlier Internet years.

We could go on and on: self-driving cars, drones that deliver packages for Amazon, buses that drive over traffic. But enough with the stats: we think you get the point. No one could have anticipated the speed at which the technological revolution would move. And this breathtaking rate of change—in all areas—will continue.

Yet, the established approaches to solving problems in many fields are based on antiquated ways of thinking. The ever-increasing changes and abundance of new information render it impossible for yesterday's solutions to solve today's problems. What may have worked to solve a problem five years ago is unlikely to work now.

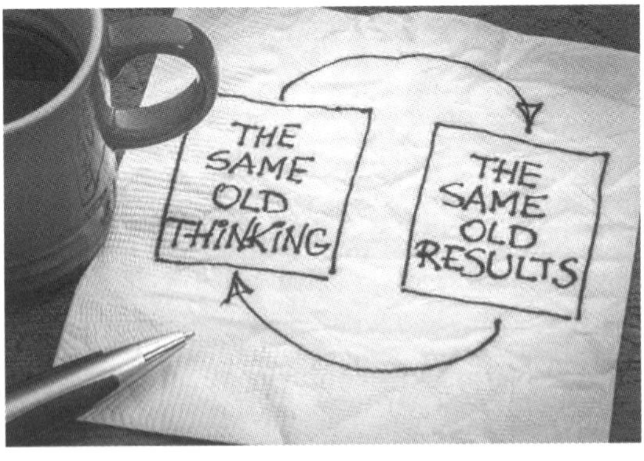

B. An Indispensable Trait

We will not succeed in navigating the complex environment of the future by peering relentlessly into a rear-view mirror. To do so, we would be out of our minds.
—Sir Ken Robinson

In light of this unprecedented rate of change, creativity has been increasingly identified as an indispensable trait. In 2010, IBM conducted a survey of more than 1,500 Chief Executive Officers from over 50 countries. According to the results of the IBM 2010 Global CEO Study, these CEOs identified creativity as the most important leadership competency for organizations to navigate the complex world that we all live in today. In fact, creativity was valued more than exactitude, organization, discipline, reliability, or vision.[1]

Many companies are encouraging creativity in the workplace. For example, Facebook has instituted a culture where every six weeks, employees are provided with an opportunity to try new ideas. Called "hackathons," they generally span 24 hours, during which hundreds of engineers confront ideas that are not within their usual work areas. These hackathons have spawned numerous marketable ideas, including Facebook's chat tool, Instagram's Hyperlapse tool, and Facebook's Safety Check.

In the progressively complex world that we now live in, creativity is an essential skill. Yesterday's solutions cannot solve all of today's problems.

C. Creativity and the Practice of Law

It is inevitable that at some point while reading this chapter you found yourself thinking, "Ok, I get it. But what does this have to do with lawyers? This isn't art school, and law isn't a creative profession."

But remember—as you learned in a prior chapter—being creative simply means that you have the ability to come up with new ideas. Good lawyers are challenged to do this all the time. Lawyers need to be creative to interpret precedent in a novel way, reframe an unfavorable fact, attempt to get a larger percentage of the pie in a negotiation, envision different theories of liability, craft innovative defenses, identify potential parties, determine how to address a jury, draft a persuasive argument in a brief, develop new means to deliver legal services, and generate alternative solutions to client problems.

As such, when solving problems, the lawyer's role is more than as a mere legal technician who simply applies the rule of law or engages in ordinary analytical skills. While a good attorney must know and comprehend the law and be particularly proficient in the technical skills of legal practice—legal analysis, legal writing, negotiation, and oral argument—that alone is not enough. As set forth in Bloom's Taxonomy, a lawyer must be able to apply, analyze, synthesize, and evaluate the law in order to solve the unique problems that clients have. A great lawyer must be creative to solve his or her client's unique problems.

In fact, the three major reports on the status of legal education underscore the importance of creativity in the practice of law. The *MacCrate Report* (1992), *Carnegie Report* (2007), and *Best Practices* (2007), all recommend that law schools put more emphasis on developing students' practice skills so that they are better equipped to engage in the practice of law upon graduating. Each of these reports recognizes the importance of creative thinking. For example, the *MacCrate Report* identifies "Generating Alternative Solutions and Strategies" as a concept that a law student should be familiar with in order to fulfill "Problem Solving," one of the 10 Fundamental Lawyering Skills. As you will read in more detail in the following chapters, divergent thinking—the ability to generate multiple solutions to a problem—is critical to creativity and creative problem solving.

You don't have to look far to find an example of creative lawyering. Consider the founding of the United States. The creative genius of Thomas Jefferson, Benjamin Franklin, Thomas Paine, John Adams, Alexander Hamilton, and others combined to create a form of government and nation never seen before. Adopted in 1787, the U.S. Constitution was innovative because it established a nation that was self-governing. In addition, it was flexible. In fact, since adoption, the U.S. Constitution has been amended 27 times. Moreover, the document incorporated an intricate plan that established a new structure of government with three branches to insure balance. The U.S. Constitution also, for the first time, created a complete process for democratic vote and amendment.

Creativity in the practice of law can also be seen in brief writing. Chief Justice John Roberts has been heralded as one of the best brief writers of all time. His brief in *Alaska v. EPA* has been identified by some as the best brief that the Justices of the United States Supreme Court have ever seen. In this case, at stake was whether Alaska or the Environmental Protection Agency would get to decide the technology that was "best" for controlling air pollution. Arguing for the state of Alaska, Justice Roberts wrote that determining the "best" technology for controlling air pollution is similar to asking people to select the "best" car: "Mario Andretti may select a Ferrari; a college student a Volkswagen beetle; a family of six a mini-van. The choices would turn on how the decision maker weighed competing priorities such as cost, mileage, safety, cargo space, speed, handling, and so on."[2]

In this passage, Justice Roberts exercised his creative muscle. Rather than falling into the abyss of endless detail about the regulations at issue, Justice Roberts compared an abstract environmental standard to the choice of a car. This analogy was effective because it was concrete and something that all readers could relate to. Moreover, it was consistent with the theme of the brief that the federal government should defer to the states. Specifically, the brief argued that the best technology to use in Alaska may not be the same as it would be in California. The next chapter elaborates on the role of analogical thinking in creativity.

D. Creativity in the United States: How Do We Measure Up?

While creativity has been consistently identified as an indispensable trait for success and competitive advantage, a 2010 study revealed a disturbing phenomenon: creativity scores in the United States are falling. How did this decline happen? As discussed in the prior chapter, everyone is born creative. As a child, you didn't see a large box as simply pieces of cardboard. Rather, you saw the numerous possibilities that the box represented: a rocket ship, playhouse, race car, or bobsled.

While no study has been conducted to determine the cause of this decline in creativity scores in the United States, there has been considerable speculation. The proliferation of technology has been identified as one cause because children are spending less time in creative endeavors like playing outside. A second speculated cause of the decline in creativity in the United States is the devaluation of creative people at home, in school, and in society. For example, at school, rather than teaching students how to think, students tend to be instructed to replicate what previous people thought. The proliferation of multiple choice tests also tends to discourage divergent thinking because this type of test encourages students to search for the one right answer. Another example of the devaluation of creativity in education in the United States is the No Child Left Behind Act ("NCLB"), which mandated standardized exams in reading/language arts and math. As a result, teachers were compelled to "teach to the test" rather than concentrate on sparking the students' ingenuity and curiosity. Unfortunately, the situation doesn't get much better in college. In 2011, a study of 2,300 college students found that many students are not being challenged to think creatively in college either.[3]

E. Creativity: Why It's Needed Now More Than Ever Checklist

- ❑ Before you read this book, did you think that it was important to be creative? Why or why not?
  - ❍ Has your opinion changed? If yes, how has it changed? If no, why not?
- ❑ Can you think of other examples that exemplify the unprecedented rate of change in society today?
- ❑ Did it surprise you that 1,500 CEOs from 50 countries identified creativity as the most important leadership competency? Why or why not?
- ❑ Can you think of an example of creative lawyering?
- ❑ Did it surprise you that creativity is declining in the United States? Why or why not?
- ❑ Reflect on the speculated causes of the decline in creativity scores in the United States. Looking back at your own upbringing and past schooling, do you relate to any of the speculated causes? Do you think these things may have impacted your creativity? For example:
  - ❍ Did your teachers "teach to the test"?
  - ❍ Did your teachers use multiple-choice questions to assess your performance?

Chapter Six

Maximizing Your Creative Potential

Creativity is the consequence of your intention to be creative and your determination to learn and use creative-thinking strategies.
—Michael Michalko, creativity expert

A prior chapter established the importance of creativity as an indispensable trait in light of the mind-bending speed of the current rate of change. And, while contrary to what you may have initially thought, lawyers need to be creative. Yet, despite the current importance of creativity, creativity in the United States is declining.

Don't fret! The good news is that you can renew and foster your creativity throughout your lifetime. While you cannot increase your inborn creative potential, you can insure that your creative potential is maximized. You can attain the traits of creative individuals, learn the creative process, and cultivate environments conducive to creativity. Like any other skill, it takes training and time to become more creative. In essence, creativity is like any other muscle—the more you use it, the more you have.

A quick reminder that our focus is on little-c creativity, otherwise known as everyday creativity. As discussed previously, everyday creativity refers to an individual's ability to solve problems that arise on a daily basis and to readily adapt to change.

While just scratching the surface, this chapter provides some tips for flexing your creative muscle in an effort to unleash your creative capacities so that you are best able to serve your clients' needs. As you will learn in an upcoming chapter, creativity is particularly important in stage 2 of the problem-solving process—Developing Options of How to Solve the Problem. The first step in maximizing your creative potential is to dispel any of the creativity myths that you read about previously. Once you have dispelled these myths, read on.

A. Become an Expert

> **STEPS TO MAXIMIZE YOUR CREATIVE POTENTIAL**
>
> - **Become an expert**
> - Adjust your attitude
> - Don't fear failure
> - Try, try again
> - Take a break
> - Think creatively
>   - Recognize that there may be more than one right answer
>   - Challenge assumptions
>   - Embrace ambiguity

Before embarking on a discussion of ways to flex your creative muscle, it is important to understand that you cannot be creative in an area until you are an expert in it. Remember that Preparation is the first stage of the creative process and involves attaining the requisite domain knowledge which is at the crux of creativity. Domain knowledge refers to the established wisdom concerning a specific area of study, including the rules, practices, and language of the particular field.

Law schools provide this domain knowledge when they teach students about substantive areas of law and the skill sets necessary for practice. The assigned cases, statutory supplements, lectures, and class discussions serve to provide the content necessary to be creative. You are also learning the skills to be able to effectively and efficiently research any issue that you may encounter. While becoming an expert may be an intimidating thought, remember that you have attained expertise in school and other areas of life. It simply takes time and practice.

The importance of domain knowledge to creativity is featured in Bloom's Taxonomy. Knowledge—the memorization of information—lies at the very bottom of the pyramid. While mastery of content may be sufficient in undergrad, representing clients requires more. The knowledge is necessary to attain the higher levels of learning that include the ability to be creative—Synthesis and Evaluation. These higher levels of learning are necessary to be able to solve the unique problems that clients pose.

B. Adjust Your Attitude

Creativity, far from requiring rare gifts and skills, depends on what you believe you can do with the talents and skills you already have.
—Tom Kelley & David Kelley, authors of *Creative Confidence*

Take a minute and answer the following question: "Are you creative?"

How did you respond? Did you immediately answer no, or did you respond in the affirmative? If you answered in the negative, you are inhibiting your creativity.

Studies have shown that people who believe that they are creative and behave as if they are creative will begin to generate creative ideas. To illustrate, in one study conducted on employees of a major publishing house, psychologists discovered that the only difference between a group of creative employees and a group of uncreative employees was attitude. Specifically, the creative employees were those that believed that they were creative, and the less creative employees believed that they were not creative. After making this discovery, the psychol-

> **STEPS TO MAXIMIZE YOUR CREATIVE POTENTIAL**
>
> - Become an expert
> - **Adjust your attitude**
> - Don't fear failure
> - Try, try again
> - Take a break
> - Think creatively
>   - Recognize that there may be more than one right answer
>   - Challenge assumptions
>   - Embrace ambiguity

ogists worked to change the belief system of the employees who did not think that they were creative. As a result of this training, within one year the less creative employees became even more creative than the original group that was identified as being creative. The change in attitude allowed these employees to flex their creative muscles in astonishing ways.

Examined in terms of the different mindsets introduced previously, you need to have a growth mindset and believe that you can increase your creative capacities through practice and experience. This is in contrast to the fixed mindset also defined in a prior chapter—a belief that creativity is a fixed commodity that you cannot change.

In his book, *Thinkertoys*, Michael Michalko, a highly acclaimed creativity expert, illustrates the impact of a person's attitude about creativity by asking the reader to read these words:

What do you read?

Invariably, you read these letters to spell "THE CAT." If you look more closely, however, you will notice that the "H" in "THE" and the "A" in "CAT" are identical. Your expectations influenced your perception of the words—you expected to read "THE," not "TAE," and "CAT" rather than "CHT." This expectation influenced your brain to see what you expected. Similarly, your expectation that you will be creative will influence your brain to be creative.[1] Your attitude determines your direction.

C. Don't Fear Failure

Failure is a bruise, not a tattoo.
—John Sinclair

One of the largest obstacles to being creative is the fear of failing. This is particularly true when you view failure as any mistake.

It is this fear of making mistakes that undermines the ability to generate new ideas.

When you look at the educational system today that is based on the premise that there is a right answer, it is not surprising that people are not comfortable with making errors. The grading system used in school serves as a clear illustration of this point. To receive an A, a student must be right over 90% of the time, and a student receives an F if they are unable to get more than 60% correct. This grading system conditions students to keep mistakes to a minimum and to fear failure.

STEPS TO MAXIMIZE YOUR CREATIVE POTENTIAL

- Become an expert
- Adjust your attitude
- **Don't fear failure**
- Try, try again
- Take a break
- Think creatively
    - Recognize that there may be more than one right answer
    - Challenge assumptions
    - Embrace ambiguity

This fear of failure is a deterrent to creativity—failure is an essential part of the creative process. Each failure allows the creator to learn what does not work. Moreover, it presents the creator with an opportunity to try a different approach.

Countless examples of successful products that arose out of the ashes of a failure exist. Instagram, a social networking app that allows users to share photographs and videos, evolved from failed efforts to create a competitor to Foursquare, the mobile check-in app that allows a person to share information about businesses and attractions around him or her. Similarly, Twitter—the online news and social networking service where users post and interact with short, 140 character messages called "tweets"—was a side-project that arose from a failed podcasting project called Odeo.

MUSEUM OF FAILURE
INNOVATION

In recognition of the role of failures in the creative process, the Museum of Failure opened in July of 2017 in Sweden. The museum showcases failed products and services from around the world in an effort to provide insight into the risky business of innovation. According to the curator, Samuel West, "We know that 80 to 90 percent of innovation projects, they fail and you never read about them," and "if there's anything we can do from these failures, is learn from them." Failed products showcased at the museum include Google Glass, the Kodak Digital Camera, and Sony Betamax.

To be creative, you must be willing to take risks. Rather than fearing failure, embrace it as simply a first attempt in learning.

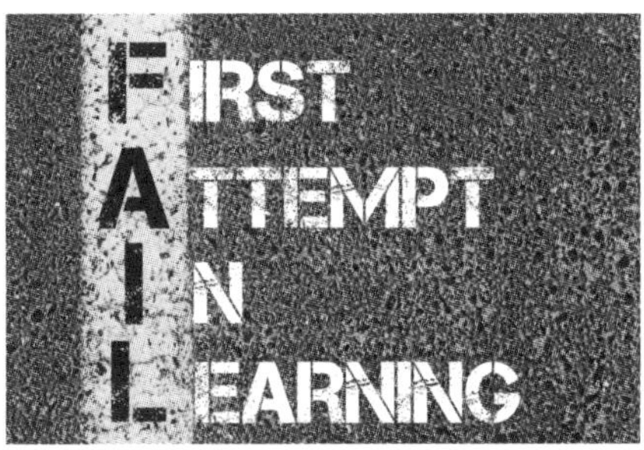

D. Try, Try Again

Grit is what allows creative geniuses to keep pressing on through failures and bad ideas in order to uncover truly valuable concepts.
—James Clear

In addition to not fearing failure, creativity requires a willingness to persevere. Contrary to popular belief, creative geniuses—those with Big-C creativity—fail all the time. But rather than letting the failures stop them, creative people and organizations persist. In other words, they are gritty. Previously, you read about the importance of grit—a characteristic that captures people's ability to persevere in the face of difficulty—for academic success. Grit is also instrumental in being creative. In fact, one study by Carol Dweck, a psychologist at Stanford, revealed that 143 creativity researchers identified resilience and perseverance as the top trait underlying the ability to be creative.[2]

> **STEPS TO MAXIMIZE YOUR CREATIVE POTENTIAL**
>
> - Become an expert
> - Adjust your attitude
> - Don't fear failure
> - **Try, try again**
> - Take a break
> - Think creatively
>   - Recognize that there may be more than one right answer
>   - Challenge assumptions
>   - Embrace ambiguity

Consider Google Glass, one of the failed products showcased at the Museum of Failure introduced above. Google Glass was a pair of glasses that functioned as a miniature wearable computer that had tremendous functionality. Despite its impressive ability to supplement human abilities with computing power, it was a failure as a consumer product because consumers believed that the glasses made the wearer look like a dork. Moreover, the glasses caused everyone around the person wearing them to feel uneasy because the user had the ability to video everything around them at all times.

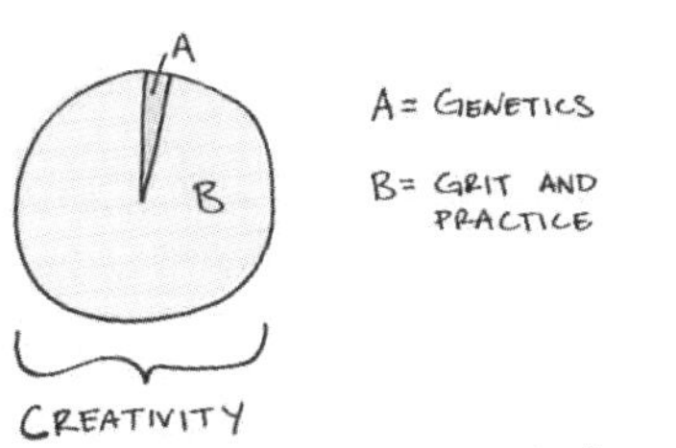

Reprinted with permission from author | JamesClear.com

It could have ended there. Google, however, didn't give up. Demonstrating grit, the company embraced the failure, learned what didn't work, and decided to take a new approach. Google changed its focus to making a

practical tool for the workplace and developed Glass Enterprise Edition ("EE"). With a focus on job productivity, EE has been very effective for factory workers who need real time access to information—with both hands free.

CREATIVE GENIUSES WHO PERSEVERED IN THE FACE OF FAILURE

- Thomas Edison invented the incandescent lightbulb—but only after learning from 1,000 failed attempts.
- Theodore Geisel's (a.k.a. Dr. Seuss) most famous book, *The Cat In The Hat*, was rejected 27 times before a publisher agreed to publish it. Currently, more than 600 million copies of his books are in print.
- Charles Goodyear worked over 30 years to invent vulcanized rubber.
- Milton Hershey started three unsuccessful candy companies in Philadelphia, Chicago, and New York before succeeding.
- J.K. Rowling, author of the *Harry Potter* books and second richest female entertainer, had her first *Harry Potter* book rejected by 12 publishers before being accepted.

Creativity takes grit, and Google was gritty. The company went from having a product that was a colossal failure to selling hundreds of units of EE to companies including the likes of General Electric, Boeing, DHL, and Volkswagen. And that's just the beginning. According to a recent Forrester Research report, over 14 million workers in the United States will wear smart glasses by 2025.[3]

In the quest to maximize your creativity, remember: take risks, embrace failure, and persevere.

七転び八起き

Fall down seven times, stand up eight.

E. Take a Break

The prior section addressed the importance of perseverance and grit in generating creative solutions to problems. Just as important as not giving up is taking a break. This is instrumental to Incubation, the second stage of the creative process that you read about in a prior chapter. During Incubation, the creator is unconsciously thinking about the problem.

STEPS TO MAXIMIZE YOUR CREATIVE POTENTIAL

- Become an expert
- Adjust your attitude
- Don't fear failure
- Try, try again
- **Take a break**
- Think creatively
  - Recognize that there may be more than one right answer
  - Challenge assumptions
  - Embrace ambiguity

In his book, *Creative Thinkering*, acclaimed creativity expert Michael Michalko illustrates the importance of taking a break through the use of the optical illusion below. Take a minute and focus on the black dot in the following illustration.

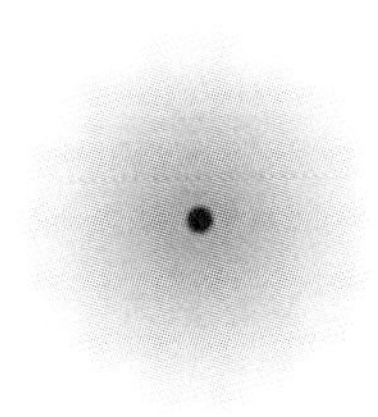

Exercise 6.1

What happened? Did the shaded background fade and disappear? This is because you were so focused on the black dot in the middle.[4]

The same thing happens when you are focusing on solving a specific problem. Concentrating on the problem that you are trying to solve can make the vague incomplete associations and pieces of disparate thoughts floating through your head—material necessary for the cognitive processes discussed below—to vanish. As you read, to be considered creative, an idea, product, service, or process need not be unprecedented. Rather, it involves, among other things, combining existing things in new ways. Taking a break allows this material to return and your mind to make connections between seemingly unrelated ideas.

One way that information can be manipulated in the Incubation stage while you are taking a break is conceptual combination. This involves combining two separate concepts in such a way that the emergent effects extend beyond the two concepts combined. The camera phone—a combination of a camera and a phone—is an example of this.

Creative ideas can also arise through conceptual transfer—the transfer of concepts from one domain to another. One form of conceptual transfer that is instrumental to creativity is analogical thinking. Analogical thinking entails transferring an idea from one context to another. Velcro is a classic example of the use of analogical thinking. After walking through a field of cockleburs that stuck to his pants, George de Mestral created Velcro—mimicking the small hooks on the burs and the loops of fabric in his pants.

Analogical thinking occurs in the law when ideas are borrowed from one area of the law to another or from another discipline. Law and economics, the application of economic theory to the analysis of law, is an example of this. The brief that Justice Roberts' wrote comparing environmental standards with the choice of a family car is another example of the use of analogical thinking in the practice of law.

Taking a break—particularly to law students and lawyers—may seem counterintuitive. Cognitive psychologists, however, have noted that it is 33% more likely that people will infer connections between distantly connected ideas after an incubation period. Nevertheless, with the many distractions in modern life discussed in a prior chapter that grab the attention of the subconscious and unconscious mind, this is the phase where people mess up the most.

This is where the mindfulness training that you read about at the beginning of the book comes in.

F. Think Creatively

While this directive makes sense, you are probably sitting there thinking, "And how do I do that? How do I learn to 'think outside the box'?" Below are a few suggestions to get you started.

1. Recognize That There May Be More Than One Right Answer

Look for the second right answer.
—Roger von Oech

Take a look at the five figures below and identify the figure that is distinct from the others.

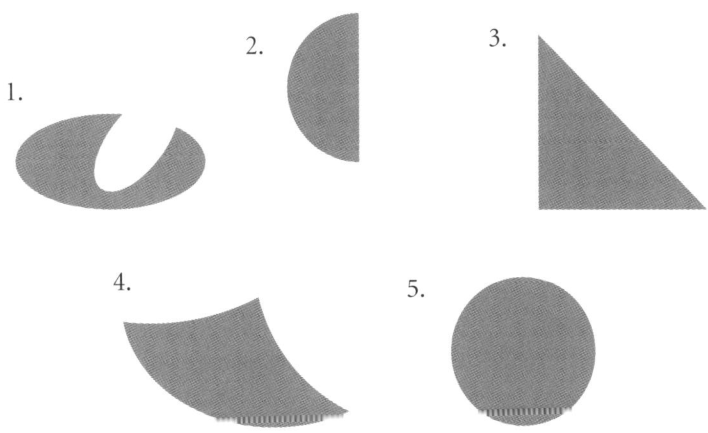

Exercise 6.2

If you selected number 2, you are correct. This is the only shape that has both a straight line and a curvy line. Did you select 1? If you did, congratulations! You are also correct. Number 1 is the only shape that is asymmetrical. In fact, they are all correct—depending upon your point of view. Number 3 is the only shape with only straight lines; number 4 looks like a protrusion of a non-Euclidean triangle into a Euclidean area; and number 5 is the only shape that does not have any points.[5]

STEPS TO MAXIMIZE YOUR CREATIVE POTENTIAL

- Become an expert
- Adjust your attitude
- Don't fear failure
- Try, try again
- Take a break
- **Think creatively**
  - **Recognize that there may be more than one right answer**
  - Challenge assumptions
  - Embrace ambiguity

To be creative, you must stop believing that there is always a right answer. This type of thinking is convergent thinking. The approach that there is a right answer has been ingrained in you throughout your schooling. In fact, one study found that the average college student will have taken more than 2,600 tests, quizzes, and exams by the time he or she graduates from college, and for each of these assessments, invariably, there was a right answer. Although convergent thinking is important in the Verification stage of the creative process, it is detrimental to generating creative solutions.

While this "right answer" approach is fine for situations where there is only one answer—math problems, for example—most of life's problems have many possible solutions. There may be many right answers to solve your client's problem—the solution will depend upon your client's unique circumstances and objectives. The real danger of believing in the existence of one right answer is that you stop looking for alternative right answers as soon as you find one. The first answer may not be the best solution for your client.

As discussed in previous chapters, divergent thinking—the ability to generate multiple solutions to a problem—is critical to creativity and creative problem solving.

So, how do you go about looking for the second right answer? The third? Fourth? Fifth? Etc.? One technique is to reframe the problem so that you are looking for multiple solutions. For example, rather than asking "What is the solution?" ask "What are the solutions?" Framing questions to solicit plural answers will force you to think a bit more deeply and come up with more than a single idea. Searching for more than a single right answer allows you to open up your imagination. Additional strategies are discussed below.

2. *Challenge Assumptions*

Assumptions are made and most assumptions are wrong.
—Albert Einstein

Take a look at the nine dots below. Without lifting the pen, try and link all nine dots with four straight lines that go through all nine dots.

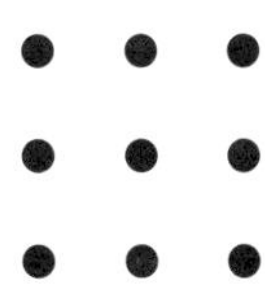

Exercise 6.3

How did you do? Were you able to solve it? If not, did you assume rules that did not in fact exist? For example, did you assume that the pen line could not extend beyond the outside dots? If so, try again. Were you able to solve the problem now that you removed that assumption? The solution is in the endnotes.[6]

This exercise illustrates that every day people make assumptions in an effort to make sense of the world. In essence, an assumption

is something that is accepted as true, without any proof, and it tends to be based on previous experiences. As seen with this exercise, an assumption serves as a barrier to creative thinking. When faced with a problem, one key to engaging in divergent thinking and generating creative solutions is to identify assumptions that you may be making. Challenging assumptions creates new perspectives about a problem and can lead to new solutions and alternatives.

Now with this in mind, without lifting the pen, link all nine dots with three straight lines that go through all nine dots. How did it go? Remember, make sure that you are not assuming rules that do not in fact exist.

Exercise 6.4

Did you get it? If not, did you assume that the lines had to go through the center of each dot? If so, try again. Were you able to solve the problem now that you removed this assumption? See the solution in the endnotes.[7]

One final query: Can you think of a way to link all nine dots with one straight line? In trying to solve this problem, list the

STEPS TO MAXIMIZE YOUR CREATIVE POTENTIAL

- Become an expert
- Adjust your attitude
- Don't fear failure
- Try, try again
- Take a break
- **Think creatively**
    - Recognize that there may be more than one right answer
    - **Challenge assumptions**
    - Embrace ambiguity

assumptions that you are making and then challenge them. Did you get it? Spoiler alert: The 9 dots can be linked in one line by cutting out the dots and putting them in a straight line.[8]

We are not suggesting that creative problem solving requires you to challenge every assumption—for example, you must adhere to the rules of professional responsibility, follow the page limits set forth in the court rules, and pay attention to the elements of a cause of action. That being said, there are numerous assumptions that you need to challenge when seeking alternative, creative solutions to a client's problem. For example, a key step in the creative problem-solving process is identifying the client's objective—whether it be compensation for loss, prevention of loss (paying damages or going to jail), vindication, or revenge. Rather than ascertaining their objectives, lawyers frequently assume the relief that their clients are seeking—which not only frustrates the clients but also forecloses creative solutions.

An experience that a law professor and two clinic students had with a client illustrate this point. The clinic represented the client on a misdemeanor charge. The police had pulled over the client—an African American undergraduate of the University of Michigan—ordered him out of his car, and requested that he submit to a pat down. The police pressed the client's face down onto the hood of the car, handcuffed him, and arrested him when the client refused to submit to the search because he claimed that it was in violation of his constitutional rights.

When the case went to trial, the prosecutor asked the judge to dismiss the case. While this may seem like a victory to the client, he was furious. Rather than asking the client what his goals were, the lawyers had assumed that the client's objective was to get rid of the misdemeanor charge. In fact, the client had wanted a public trial to restore his reputation and his dignity.[9]

Accordingly, when working to creatively solve a client's problem, one approach is to begin by listing the assumptions that you are making about the problem. Are you assuming the client's objectives? The cause(s) of action that can be brought? The potential parties to the case? The facts? Next, try reversing each assumption. For example, if you are assuming that the client wants to go to trial, the reverse may be to settle before filing any documents with the court. Next, ask yourself how to accomplish each reversal. Finally, select one and work on making it a realistic idea.

3. Embrace Ambiguity

Looking for the second right answer and challenging assumptions are two considerations when generating creative solutions to a problem. These are closely tied to another key aspect of creativity—embracing ambiguity. Tolerance of ambiguity refers to your ability to remain open-minded when facing an ambiguous situation, one that you can interpret in more than one way.

STEPS TO MAXIMIZE YOUR CREATIVE POTENTIAL

- Become an expert
- Adjust your attitude
- Don't fear failure
- Try, try again
- Take a break
- **Think creatively**
  - Recognize that there may be more than one answer
  - Challenge assumptions
  - **Embrace ambiguity**

The drawing above is a well-known visual model of ambiguity. This drawing—known as the "duck-rabbit" picture—can be seen as either a duck or a rabbit, just not at the same time. The duck is facing towards the left-hand margin and the rabbit is facing towards the right-hand margin.

Psychologists have developed standard questionnaires like the one below to gauge a person's comfort level with ambiguity. Before you move on, please circle your responses to the following statements:

I prefer addressing problems that have straightforward answers.	TRUE	FALSE
I am uncomfortable breaking rules.	TRUE	FALSE
I think that a distinct difference exists between right and wrong.	TRUE	FALSE
The most rewarding thing about working on a problem is solving it.	TRUE	FALSE
I think that almost every situation is viewed best from one perspective.	TRUE	FALSE

How many times did you circle "FALSE"? The more "FALSEs" you circled, the higher your tolerance for ambiguity.[10]

Studies have shown that creative individuals are tolerant of ambiguity. They are able to function well in uncertain situations. This tolerance for ambiguity is important because it enables a person to see the world from different perspectives. People that are tolerant of ambiguity have an easier time dealing with imprecise problems that have creative potential. The tendency to embrace strange or unknown situations, rather than be frightened by them, enables an individual to respond creatively.

Unfortunately, people tend to want to avoid ambiguity because situations that can be interpreted in more than one way are confusing. This mindset is a good one in situations where precision, clarity, and specificity are important, such as when drafting a contract. To be creative, however, fight the desire to impose order in the messy world we live in. Instead, seek out the ambiguities. Change your perspective in an effort to see things differently. As you will read in a later chapter, you will need to develop a tolerance of ambiguity to solve your clients' problems.

Let's take a look at a few problems that help to illustrate this point and demonstrate how to work towards embracing ambiguities and seeing things differently.

Take a look at the illustration below. How could you remove 3 matches to make 4?

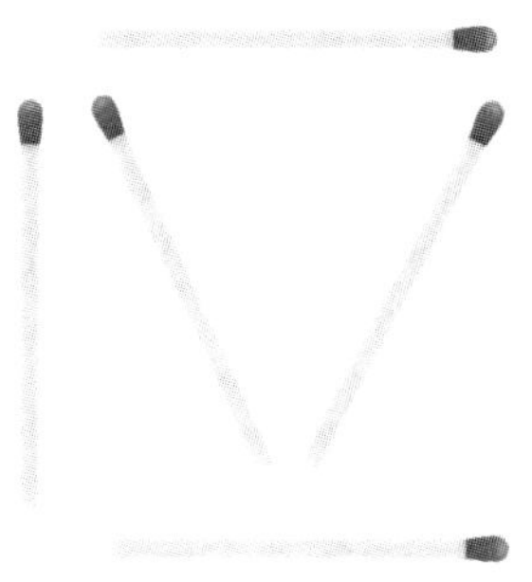

Exercise 6.5

At first look, it appears that this problem has no obvious solution: 6 minus 3 can't equal 4. Look for ambiguities and ask yourself some questions—"Are there other ways to make 4?" "Can 4 be something else?" To solve the problem, simply remove the matches located at the top, bottom, and right—leaving you with IV, the Roman numeral for 4.[11]

Sticking with matches for now, solve this equation of Roman numerals made with ten matches. Currently, the equation is incorrect. Correct the equation without touching the matches, adding new matches, or taking away any matches.

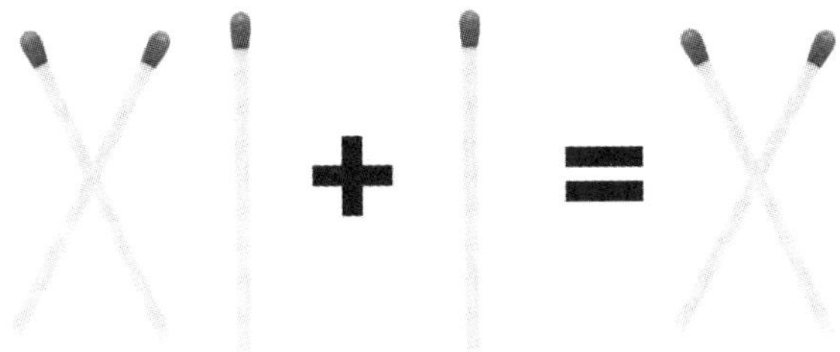

Exercise 6.6

Stumped? Once again, to solve this problem you need to embrace the uncertainty and change the way you are looking at it. To correct the equation, turn the book upside down.[12]

Last one.

What is one-half of thirteen?

Exercise 6.7

Take a few minutes to generate responses—remembering to consider the least obvious as well as the most likely approaches and answers.

Most people immediately answer 6½. While correct, this isn't the only answer. Other answers include, but are not limited to:

Answer	Explanation
6.5	13 divided in half
1 & 3	1|3. 13 split in half between the 1 and the 3.
Thir|teen	Thirteen split in half with 4 letters on each side
11 & 2	The Roman numeral for 13—XIII—divided in half is XI|II or 11 and 2
8	The Roman numeral for 13 halved horizontally leaves a Roman numeral 8—~~XIII~~.[1]

To develop creative solutions to client problems, rather than getting anxious, embrace the ambiguity. Change your perspective. Try asking yourself the following questions: "What's going on here?" "What does this mean?" "How else can it be interpreted?" "What would the judge's perspective be?" "What would the opposing party's perspective be?" Tolerating ambiguity and considering various perspectives will allow you to keep an open mind and be receptive to novel ideas that may lead to creative solutions. The legal example in the next part of this chapter demonstrates the importance of being tolerant of ambiguity in the practice of law.

G. Putting It All Together

As you have invariably noticed, the considerations discussed above about how to be creative overlap considerably. By necessity, these skills do not stand in isolation. The following legal example illustrates how the tips for flexing your creative muscle were used in a legal context to solve a client's problem.

In this case, a small law firm was hired to defend a client's trademark rights. A Fortune 500 company was suing the client for trademark infringement. A trademark is a word, symbol, or phrase, that a seller or manufacturer uses to identify its products and differentiate them from another seller's products. The Nike swoosh and phrase "Just Do It" are examples of trademarks.

In this case, both parties used the same trademark, and the services involved were nearly identical. The Fortune 500 company claimed that it had acquired rights to the trademark because it had used the trademark first and the client was infringing on the trademark because the client's trademark would likely cause consumer confusion.

Accordingly, the case came down to priority of use. In essence, pursuant to the priority of use doctrine, whoever uses the trademark first usually wins, particularly when the trademarks and the goods or services used by the two parties are extremely similar. Therefore, under conventional defense methods, the Fortune 500 company was the winner.

Rather than throwing in the towel, the firm flexed its creative muscle. The firm decided to think outside the box and see if they could find someone else who had priority of use associated with the trademark that preceded the use by the Fortune 500 company. Lo and behold, the firm located a company that had been using an identical trademark for 50 years. The firm's client purchased the company—the company had been considering closing—and acquired the trademark rights. The trademark rights acquired included the priority of use date prior to that of the Fortune 500 company's first use date. The case then quickly settled.[13]

When the traditional defense didn't work, the firm flexed its creative muscle. The firm displayed a creative attitude, took risks, and persevered. Rather than assuming one right answer, the firm challenged assumptions and embraced ambiguities. The firm looked at the issue from a different perspective and generated a creative solution to its client's problem.

H. Maximizing Your Creative Potential Checklist

- ❑ If you answered the question "Are you creative?" in the negative, reflect on why you responded this way. Think about ways you can work towards changing your attitude.
- ❑ Think about a time that you took a risk, and it didn't work out the way you wanted it to. What happened? How did you deal with it?
- ❑ Can you think of a time where you struggled with a task or problem? Did you give up? If so, think about why you gave up and how to improve your grit.
- ❑ Think back to the exercises in the discussion about how to think creatively. How did you do? Did you find that you:
    - ❍ Assumed one right answer?
    - ❍ Made assumptions that were not stated?
    - ❍ Were confused and unsettled by any ambiguities?

You read about strategies for maximizing your creative potential. The next time you are asked to solve a problem, use the following checklist to evaluate how well you have been able to flex your creative muscle.

- ❑ Did you have the requisite domain knowledge? If not, what did you do to attain it?
- ❑ Did you have a creative attitude? Did you believe that you could generate creative solutions to the problem?
- ❑ Were you willing to take risks or did the fear of failure become an obstacle to generating novel solutions?
- ❑ Did you give up quickly or did you persevere, embracing failures as a first attempt in learning?
- ❑ Did you take a break to allow your mind to unconsciously work on the problem?
- ❑ Did you stop with the first solution that you generated, or did you continue to generate additional "right answers"?

- ❑ While working to solve the problem, did you stop to identify any assumptions that you may have been making? Did you challenge those assumptions, where appropriate?
- ❑ When faced with uncertainty, did you embrace ambiguity and seek to see the problem from different perspectives?

Part IV

Being a Legal Problem Solver

"I have a problem." You try to focus as you listen to a person sitting across the table from you who has come to you with a problem. Your phone vibrates in your pocket, alerting you to incoming texts. You realize you have another meeting that morning you have to prepare for, and you glance at the stack of files on your desk that you need to review before lunch. You take a sip of your coffee and remember you are trying to cut back on caffeine and wonder when you will fit in the run you planned for today. You glance at your computer screen and see emails you need to respond to. A silence fills the room and your attention goes back to the person telling you her story as you realize she is waiting for your response after she asks you what she should do about the biggest problem she is facing in her life.

Wait, what did she just tell you? The story she relayed to you seems incomplete and ambiguous. She seems very upset and you are not sure how to proceed. You are not sure if you missed it, but she didn't tell you the legal issue or tell you what she wants to do to solve the problem. She may have even left out some critical facts. You glance up at your framed law school diploma on your office wall, start breaking a sweat, your heart pounding, and think—did law school prepare me for how to solve a client's problem?

In law school, classes focused on one area of law, such as Contracts, Torts, or Property, at a time. Could this person's problem involve more than one area of the law? Also, law school hypotheticals and cases didn't seem to involve real people. You didn't seem to focus on clients—you can't remember ever meeting one—it was more academic, preparing in case you got called on by your professor. You were more concerned with doing well on your exams than on actual clients.

Is this woman you just met even your client yet? Did you just create an attorney-client relationship? What does your client want? How do you proceed?

You learned in a previous part of the book why training your brain to be mindful has numerous benefits, and how thinking creatively can lead to better solutions; now let's turn to a systematic approach to problem solving. No matter what the legal setting, issue, or client, understanding and applying a problem-solving methodology helps lawyers maximize their potential to successfully achieve the client's objectives.

This part of the book will break down a problem-solving methodology into stages. The problem-solving methodology discussed in this book is based on the problem-solving methodology developed by Joseph William Singer and Todd D. Rakoff of Harvard Law School.[1] After providing an overview of problem solving, each chapter will focus on a different stage. You will also see how mindfulness and creativity play a role in the stages and why lawyers are problem solvers.

Chapter Seven

Stages of Problem Solving

While the focus in most law school courses may be on how a court resolved a case at the end of a dispute, in legal practice, the focus is on the client, often at the beginning of a case, when the problem is first presented. The lawyer's role is to help the client resolve or avoid a problem, often with incomplete facts and imperfect information. In practice, you are no longer reading a hypothetical situation about a fictitious client or a client that only appears on a page. Whether you are representing an indigent client or a billion-dollar international corporation, you have a responsibility to serve your client. While law schools develop your ability to think like a lawyer, learning and applying a systematic approach to problem solving develops your ability to think like a client and transforms your understanding of lawyering.

A. Lawyers Are Problem Solvers

To be a problem-solving lawyer, you must appreciate the process of problem solving in the real world. This process involves applying a problem-solving methodology in a pragmatic way in practical dilemmas that focus on the client. Problem solving involves connecting legal knowledge, theory, and skills to help achieve a client's objectives, after carefully considering options and strategies and making judgments about the most appropriate solution. When approaching a problem, lawyers should be mindful to solve the client's problem creatively.

Problem solving is a journey with several stages. To effectively and efficiently solve a problem, you should approach problem solving as a fluid and recursive process. Going through different

stages of problem solving and asking the right questions is critical to understand a client's problem, help solve it, prevent it from getting worse, or avoid it. Many steps, models, or methodologies for problem solving exist. A common theme among them is that problem solving involves some form of the following stages: identify the problem, develop options, evaluate the options, generate and implement a plan, and then reflect on the solution.

STAGES OF PROBLEM SOLVING

- Identify the problem
- Develop options
- Evaluate the options
- Generate and implement a plan
- Reflect on the solution

Hold on. Before embarking on the stages of problem solving, remember to apply a mindful approach to solve a problem with intention. Use mindfulness, as discussed in an earlier part of this book, to sharpen or train your brain to focus on problem solving. Set your intention when you first sit down to try to solve your client's problem. Setting your intention means establishing a goal for a particular stage of problem solving. It may be identifying the legal issues involved, identifying your client, or gathering all the relevant facts. You may be thinking, "I don't have time to do this, I need to jump in and solve this problem quickly." Setting your intention won't take long and will help you solve the problem purposefully, preventing you from diving in and spinning your wheels randomly, without direction. Consider what you are doing and why. Mindfully working to solve a client's problem may also improve decision making by reducing your stress and improving your concentration.

Once you've set your intention in the problem-solving process, clear your mind to enable you to mindfully accomplish it. Try a breathing exercise or quick burst of physical exercise to clear your mental space as discussed in the mindfulness section of this book. When trying to focus, it is okay if thoughts keep popping into your head. Don't be judgmental or dwell on those thoughts. Just return to your intention. Write those thoughts down and deal with them later after you complete the task in front of you. By writing them down, you won't forget them and you can focus on your intention.

To follow through with your mindful intention when solving a client's problem, next make sure you are working in a physical space that is distraction-free. Do you need a space that allows you to spread out files and materials? Have only the resources you need in front of you to allow you to focus. Do you only need a computer? Put your phone physically away and turn off Internet access if possible or disconnect any distracting alerts, emails, or social media postings.

Try disconnecting for a time period you set, such as 55 minutes; then, take a set time period break of about five minutes to check your email, texts, and social media, then go back to work. Consider what, if anything, undermines your ability to solve a problem. At first, being disconnected may seem difficult, but you will see how you will be more focused on solving the client's problem without distractions. Now you are ready to begin.

B. Stages of Problem Solving Checklist

❑ What are the stages of problem solving?

❑ Before beginning to work on solving your client's problem, have you taken the time to set your intention?

❑ Have you cleared your physical space to eliminate distractions and maintain your focus on problem solving?

Chapter Eight

Identify the Problem

The first stage of problem solving is recognizing that there is a problem or potential problem your client is facing or could be facing. Recognizing the problem includes identifying your client and determining the relevant facts. This stage is similar to spotting the issues in a law school hypothetical or exam and keying in on the outcome-determinative facts.

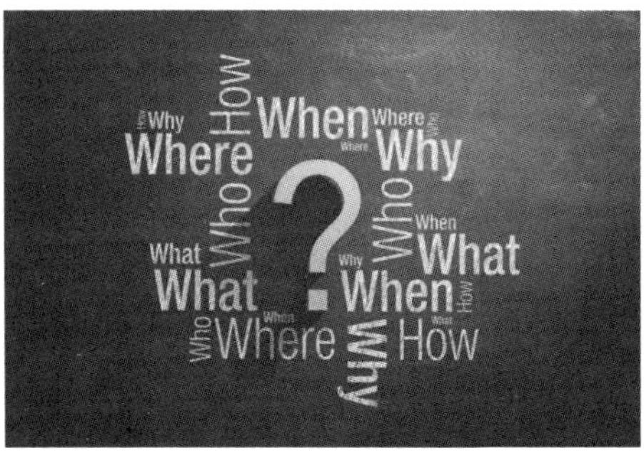

A. Identify the Client

You never really understand a person until you consider things from his point of view ... Until you climb into his skin and walk around in it.
—Atticus Finch

Problem solving is a client-centered practice, yet clients are often absent in the law school curriculum. Whenever solving a problem, your focus should be on the client you represent; it is the core pursuit of the legal profession. Interact with your client as a person, not a problem to be solved. Remember, as a lawyer, you are acting on behalf of a client.

> **STAGES OF PROBLEM SOLVING**
>
> - **Identify the problem**
>   - **Identify the client**
>   - Determine the facts
> - Develop options
> - Evaluate the options
> - Generate and implement a plan
> - Reflect on the solution

What is it like to be a client? Lawyers can best serve clients if they keep that in mind. Ideally, every lawyer should first experience what it is like to be a client. Have you ever hired a lawyer? If so, did your lawyer work with you effectively to solve your problem? What did the lawyer do, or not do, to foster an effective working relationship with you as the client? Having a first-hand experience as a client gives you a client's perspective.

Before anything is done to solve a problem, to keep focus on the client, consider who your client is. Once you identify your client, evaluate what you know about your client. The identification of your client may affect your representation. Identifying your client may be obvious in some cases, but not clear in others. For example, a client may be an individual, government entity, or a corporation. You also may have more than one client.

In addition to thinking about who your client is, keep in mind your relationship with others involved in the case and potential future cases, such as parties, witnesses, potential audiences, stakeholders, your boss, your employer, the opposing attorney, the judge, and any relevant agencies involved. As will be discussed later, in the part of the book that examines ethical concerns, avoid representing a client with interests that may conflict with the interests of another client.

Also think about whether a lawyer-client relationship even exists yet. In some situations, it may be unclear whether a lawyer-client relationship has even formed. Once you attend law school, it may seem like everyone you know, family, friend, acquaintance, or stranger, may casually ask for your advice about a problem. Consider whether the person who asked for your help with a problem thinks or could think a lawyer-client relationship has formed. As discussed later in this book, you need to check the rules of professional responsibility in your jurisdiction to see when a lawyer-client relationship exists. If a person seeking your advice to her problem perceives the formation of a lawyer-client relationship, that perception could impact confidentiality and potential malpractice. Be cautious when casually asked for legal advice. Make clear whether you are representing the person as one of your clients.

B. Determine the Facts

Lawyers do more than draft legal documents, they develop and investigate facts. Do not just rely on the facts of a problem relayed by a client or ignore critical facts. Investigate more facts if needed. Also, evaluate the reliability and significance of the information. There is a difference between facts and inferences. Lawyers focus on the facts that they can prove.

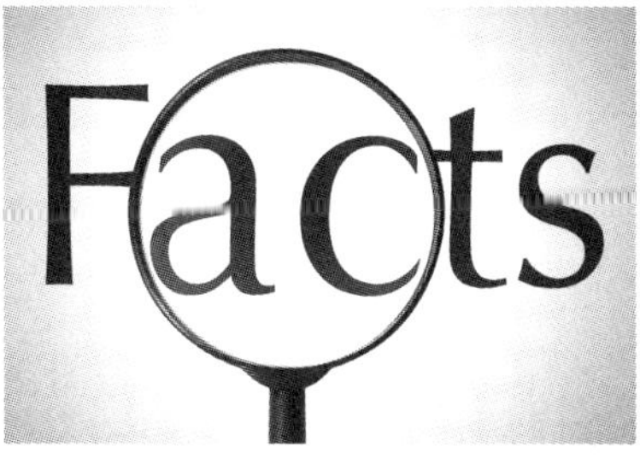

Where do facts come from? From what source? The facts in law school exams, hypotheticals, or judicial opinions may seem to only exist on a page. In practice, facts do not come from a book and often must be developed. They are often ambiguous, and good problem solvers have to develop a tolerance for ambiguity.

Although in law school students often focus on legal research, factual research may be just as important as the law when faced with a client's problem. Don't fall down the rabbit hole of legal research without spending the same effort on identifying all the critical facts. Knowing what you don't know and asking the right questions can be just as important as the facts initially presented. A client's description of her problem may include facts that are messy, confusing, conflicting, and incomplete that require further exploration. Consider the reliability, source, and significance of the facts. The client may not be purposefully withholding information but may be embarrassed, scared, confused, or unaware of what could be relevant. What possible motivation or agenda do clients, witnesses, parties, and others have in describing the facts?

STAGES OF PROBLEM SOLVING

- **Identify the problem**
  - Identify the client
  - **Determine the facts**
- Develop options
- Evaluate the options
- Generate and implement a plan
- Reflect on the solution

To solve a problem, a lawyer may have to determine how to further research, gather, develop, or investigate the facts. Facts can be developed in numerous ways, such as: reviewing documents, such as a contract or lease, emails, notes from a client meeting, or pictures; talking and listening to the client, witnesses, or other parties in the case; or visiting the location of the problem to collect or confirm facts. Lawyers must employ active listening skills, encourage communication, and convey empathetic understanding. A mindfulness practice may also increase your empathy for clients, help you stay client focused, and lead to more satisfied clients. It is critical to confirm what facts are known as well as recognize what facts are unknown, unclear, or underdeveloped, including what is said and what is not said. Taking the time to stop and mindfully listen to the client will help you connect with the client, thereby enabling a more empathetic relationship.

When trying to uncover facts, remember that the fiduciary relationship between lawyer and client demands trust and confidence. Lawyers need to be respectful and build a rapport with their client. A lawyer's instinct when a client asks for help with a problem may be to jump to legal options to solve it, but first, the lawyer must remember to listen and be empathetic. Keep an open mind about what facts could be relevant. Practicing mindfulness will increase the amount of information you gather by being aware, observant, and non-judgmental. Offering your time and attention, and being willing to listen, can go a long way.

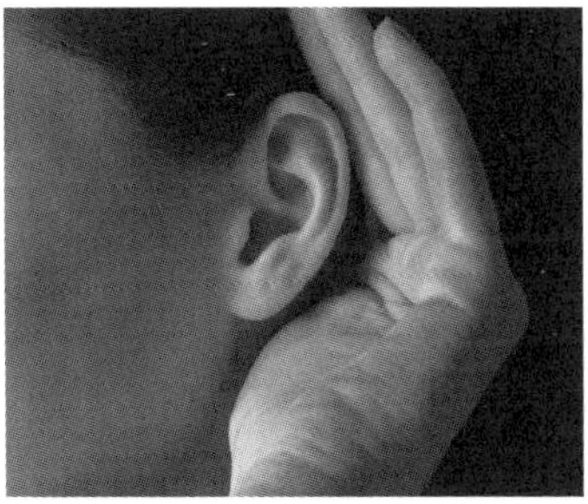

Sometimes when people come to you with a problem,
the best thing you can do is listen.
—Dear Abby

The facts of a problem need to be fully developed to brainstorm various options of how to solve the problem. Determine the simplest, most efficient and cost-effective way to learn the facts without making the problem worse. Don't be impatient. Let clients tell their story, guiding them when necessary but avoid interrupting them too much. A chronological account of the events related to the client's problem may promote memory recall.

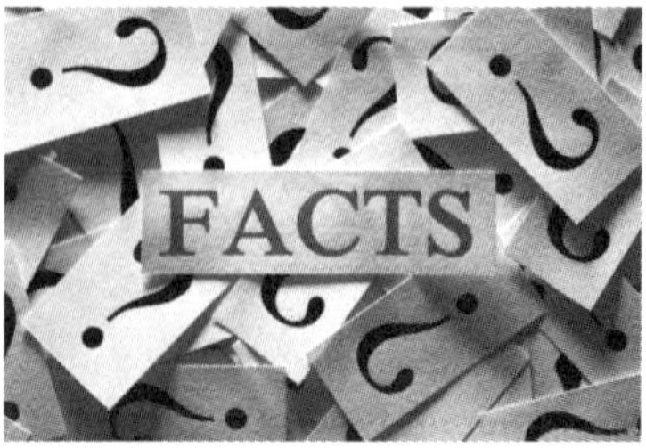

Think about using techniques to encourage the client to give a full account of the problem. Use a combination of different types of questions, such as open and closed questions. Be careful to avoid moving too quickly from open questions to closed questions. Get the whole story first and try not to inhibit the free flow of information or sound like you are cross-examining the client.

Examples of open questions include, "please tell me about your problem that has led you to seek my advice," or "describe ..." or "explain...." Open questions allow a broad response. Open questions can uncover the who, what, where, when, why, and how, related to the client's problem. They encourage clients to talk, which can be useful at the beginning of a meeting. They allow lawyers to maximize information and build trust and rapport with a client. Open questions, however, may be problematic if a client can't focus on the topic.

Closed questions are more restrictive and invite a specific response, such as yes/no or a short answer. Closed questions can be leading questions that suggest the answer, such as "you were at the theatre that night, right?" This type of question can be effective by making the client feel more comfortable in admitting facts that may be embarrassing.

Follow up questions and summarizing questions can be effective to use. Follow up questions, such as "what did you mean when you said...," communicate that you are paying attention and want to explore and understand a client's response, but does not suggest an answer. Summarizing questions, such as paraphrasing the client's story, can be useful at the end to invite the client to elaborate, clarify, or verify information.

Be aware of any inhibitors of communication that may affect development of the facts. Pay attention to a client's, as well as your own, verbal and nonverbal cues when communicating, such as: tone, volume, pace, eye contact, body language, and facial expressions. Barriers to communication could include: fear, embarrassment, stress, confusion, social norms, or implicit bias. Implicit bias refers to unconscious views, beliefs, attitudes, or preferences, such as those related to race, sexual orientation, gender, or disability, just to name a few.

When developing the facts of a problem, recognize any possible cultural issues. An awareness of the importance of cultural competency and its significance can help you identify any culturally sensitive issues that may affect the critical facts or their application to the law. Cultural competency can lead to a better outcome for your client. Consider whether you are making any assumptions, inferences, opinions, or have any implicit biases. Keep in mind problem solving can be global and involve cultural competency or cultural intelligence.

Problem solving effectively includes cultural competency. Consider how cultural issues could play a role in the following scenarios:

- A defendant argues he cannot confront his accuser because she wears a burka and refuses to remove it.
- A dispute involves two neighbors. One claims negligent infliction of emotional distress inflicted by another neighbor over political signs posted in her yard.
- A family celebrating Kwanzaa decorates their house and yard with colorful art and plays loud music, and is being sued for denial of quiet enjoyment, a nuisance tort.
- Two contracting parties have a potential imbalance in race, gender, education, and economic status, and one tries to argue the contract is invalid.
- An old man gives a substantial amount of money to a younger woman as a gift, and his family claims undue influence.

C. Identify the Problem Checklists

1. Identify the Client Checklist

- ❑ Who is the client?
    - ❍ Is it an individual, government entity, or a corporation?
    - ❍ Is there more than one?
- ❑ What do you know about your client (education, work, family, age, health, prior legal experience, life experience, risk tolerance, resources, time)?

2. Determine the Facts Checklist

- ❑ What facts do you know?
    - ❍ Who?
        - Who are the interested parties?
        - Who are the witnesses?
        - Who have you talked to about the facts?
    - ❍ What happened?
    - ❍ When?
    - ❍ Where?
    - ❍ Why?
    - ❍ How?
- ❑ From what source do the facts come?
    - ❍ Have you evaluated the reliability and significance of the information?
    - ❍ What possible motivation, agenda, or perspective do the client, witness, parties, or others have in describing the facts?
    - ❍ Are you making any assumptions or inferences?
- ❑ What facts do you not yet know?
    - ❍ How will you find them out or gather missing facts?

- ❑ Have you used a combination of open and closed questions to uncover facts?
- ❑ Have you established a rapport with your client? How?
- ❑ Have you engaged in active listening?
- ❑ Have you considered cultural issues, implicit bias, diversity, and inclusion issues that may affect the facts or how the law applies to those facts?

Chapter Nine

Develop Options

> **STAGES OF PROBLEM SOLVING**
> - Identify the problem
>   - Identify the client
>   - Determine the facts
> - **Develop options**
>   - Identify the client's objectives
>   - Recognize the legal challenges and opportunities
>   - Recognize the ethical and moral concerns
>   - Consider creative solutions
>   - Collaborate
> - Evaluate the options
> - Generate and implement a plan
> - Reflect on the solution

Problem solving often does not result in one obvious correct answer of how to proceed. Do not let the perfect be the enemy of the good. Practicing mindfulness and using creative thinking allows you to generate multiple possible options instead of just obvious ones. Rather than focusing prematurely on unconscious reactions and thoughts that may lead to narrow choices, be mindful and creative.

Remember the concepts discussed in an earlier part of this book involving divergent thinking, convergent thinking, and analogical thinking. Divergent thinking includes mental processes that allow a person to generate multiple possible solutions to a problem by thinking outside of the box. Convergent thinking is the opposite of divergent thinking. It is more evaluative, thinking inside the box. Convergent thinking is often used to give a "correct" answer to a standard question, such as on a test in school. Analogical thinking involves seeing and making connections between the boxes.

In the brainstorming stage, don't evaluate ideas at the same time you are generating solutions to the problem. Just as you should not edit while you write, generating ideas and evaluating ideas at the same time involves mental switches that take time and energy. As discussed in the mindfulness part of this book, focus on one task at a time; forget about multitasking. Think of employing "monotasking."

Think critically and creatively and recognize that a legal solution may not be the best one. Remember to stay focused on the client, not what you would do in the client's shoes. There may be challenges and opportunities the law presents as well as ethical and moral issues that arise. You may need to advise a client to choose between options, none of which may seem good. Or you may need to discuss an option the client may not want to hear but that you have to discuss to fully inform your client. Always keep in mind the client's objectives. Finally, collaboration can lead to the development of alternative options that you may not have thought of if you were working alone.

A. Identify the Client's Objectives

When developing options of how to solve a client's problem, it is of utmost importance to determine what the client's objectives are. Listen to clients, keeping in mind their ultimate objectives. What clients say they want their lawyer to do may not be the best way for them to achieve their objectives. By first focusing on clients' priorities and objectives, a lawyer can help determine the best options and how to proceed to solve clients' problems.

STAGES OF PROBLEM SOLVING

- Identify the problem
  - Identify the client
  - Determine the facts
- **Develop options**
  - **Identify the client's objectives**
  - Recognize the legal challenges and opportunities
  - Recognize the ethical and moral concerns
  - Consider creative solutions
  - Collaborate
- Evaluate the options
- Generate and implement a plan
- Reflect on the solution

Position (*what*) v. Interest (*why*)

You should spend a significant amount of time fleshing out a client's objectives during problem solving. A lawyer may need to help clients clarify their objectives. Confusion or uncertainty of the lawyer or client regarding the client's objectives can hinder effective problem solving.

Consider the difference between your client's position and interest.[1] The client's position is *WHAT* she says she wants as the outcome. The client's interest is *WHY* she wants it, i.e., the reason why the outcome is important to her.

For an illustration of the difference between position and interest, consider the example involving two chefs who found only one orange left in the kitchen.[2] Both chefs stated they wanted the orange for a dish they needed to prepare. Who should get the orange? What is the solution?

What if the chefs divide the orange and each get half? Is this the best solution? It depends. Famous lawyer answer, right? Why do they need the orange? One chef needed the juice of the orange for a sauce; the other chef needed the orange's peel for a cake batter. Half an orange would not be enough for either purpose. What is the better solution? Both chefs could use the same orange: one chef squeezes the juice from the orange for her sauce and the other chef uses the peel. While their positions (what they wanted, i.e. the orange) seemed opposing at first, after considering their interests (why they wanted the orange, which ended up being for different reasons), the best solution was reached.

SMART

S: **S**pecific
M: **M**easurable
A: **A**ttainable
R: **R**elevant
T: **T**imely

In addition to thinking about interests and goals, consider whether a client's goals are SMART:[3] Specific, Measurable, Attainable, Relevant, and Timely.

Is the client's objective a specific one that is more likely to get accomplished versus a general one? If a client says she wants to get out of trouble with the law, being more specific is more helpful to make sure the proposed solution truly meets her goal. An example of a more specific objective is she does not want to have a permanent record. Another example is when a client says he wants to spend more time with his children in a custody dispute. A more specific objective of seeing his children three times a week is more helpful.

Also, to determine if a client's objective has been met or progress is being made towards reaching it, consider whether it is measurable. If a client tells you he wants to get rich, it is not as effective as stating a specific dollar figure he wants for damages. If a client says he wants remorse shown, a more measurable objective would be to ask for an apology.

Also, determine whether the objective is attainable. Managing a client's expectations is important in the problem-solving process. The client must be honest with herself and with you about what is realistic. If the client wants to continue to practice medicine but has lost her license to practice, her goal may not be attainable. Thus, she may need to adjust her objective.

Next, consider whether the client's objective is relevant at the time you are trying to solve the problem. Should a solution be implemented and if so, why? For example, if a client has not been sued yet but only faces the threat of a lawsuit, should a client respond to that threat?

Finally, review whether the client has a timely objective. Does immediate action need to be taken? When should action be taken? What would happen if no action was taken?

Also, if a client has more than one objective or if objectives conflict, a lawyer may need to help the client prioritize them. A lawyer needs to review all types of goals: short-term, long-term, financial, emotional, personal, moral, religious, political, psychological, and legal.

In addition to determining what a client wants, a lawyer should consider what the client does not want. Determine how risk averse your client is to attain her objectives. A client's aversion to risk may affect how you proceed as well as how you can help your client achieve her objectives within the bounds of the law.

Lawyers must focus on the client's objectives, not their own objectives, self-interest, preconceived notions, bias, or aversion to risk. A lawyer may also need to adjust the client's expectations about what can be done to solve the client's problem. Being clear on what the client wants the outcome to be is important before deciding on a course of action.

B. Understand the Relevant Law and How It Could Apply

In addition to identifying the client's objectives, in order to develop options of how to solve a client's problem, consider the relevant law and how it could apply to your client's problem. What does the law allow? What does the law restrict? What plausible arguments could be made looking at a client's problem from both sides?

STAGES OF PROBLEM SOLVING

- Identify the problem
  - Identify the client
  - Determine the facts
- **Develop options**
  - Identify the client's objectives
  - **Understand the relevant law and how it could apply**
  - Recognize the ethical and moral concerns
  - Consider creative solutions
  - Collaborate
- Evaluate the options
- Generate and implement a plan
- Reflect on the solution

You need to understand the legal system, sources of the law, and their relationships to each other. In law school, you may work on problems in silos dedicated to one specific area of the law, such as Contracts, Torts, or Property, while practice may involve more complex problems. A client's problem may involve multiple issues, spanning several different areas of the law. You may need to engage in simple legal research or more complex legal research to determine the law relevant to your client's problem. After finding relevant authority, make sure to read it critically to understand and assess its significance. Consider the policies behind the law as well.

When reviewing the law, understand the procedural postures and burdens of proof. Which party has the burden of proof? What is the appropriate standard of review? Is there any legal proceeding yet in your client's case? Maybe your client has not yet been named in a lawsuit or perhaps court proceedings have not even begun and are merely threatened.

Synthesize the legal sources, including reconciling possible conflicting authority and evaluate its validity. There is inherent uncertainty in the law and, thus, uncertainty in problem solving. For example, in a problem involving a covenant not to compete, the law may restrict a former employee's ability to work elsewhere for a reasonable time. The law, however, may not specifically define what is reasonable.

When applying the law to your client's problem, use different forms of legal reasoning you learned in your legal writing classes, such as inductive, deductive, policy-based, or narrative reasoning. Lawyers may use more than one type of reasoning when problem solving. For a legal example utilizing these types of reasoning, consider the following. You research the relevant law in the jurisdiction of your client's problem and find binding primary authority—a statute that prohibits driving a motor vehicle on a public way while intoxicated. Your client was driving a Segway on a public way while intoxicated. Is your client guilty of violating this law? An uncertainty exists regarding the definition of a motor vehicle. If the statute provided a definition of motor vehicle, you could employ deductive reasoning and apply your client's facts, driving a Segway, to that definition. If the statute does not provide a definition of motor vehicle, you could analogize to the facts in prior decisions using analogical reasoning. What if there was a case where someone was driving a golf cart while intoxicated and was exonerated? You would want to look at the reasoning in that precedent and apply it to your client's case. You could also use the policies underlying the statute to see if driving a Segway was meant to be prohibited. Finally, you could use narrative reasoning to tell the story of why and how your client was driving a Segway and what impact the resolution of this case would have on your client and future cases.

The law may not account for every possible situation that occurs after the law was created, but it may shape your client's rights and responsibilities. Understanding the law and how it applies to your client's problem can help you make an informed decision of how to proceed to solve a client's problem; however, keep in mind the law may provide a place to start, but not an end. Consider thinking about the law and its application creatively as discussed earlier in this book. Is the root or cause of a client's problem legal? Consider whether a legal solution is the best solution to meet the client's goals. Are there nonadversarial solutions possible? Is litigation the answer? What nonlegal solutions could best serve the client? What would be the least expensive and most efficient solution?

Evaluating solutions to a client's problem doesn't end with just considering what the law allows and restricts. A client may not want to take action that proceeds right up to the limits of the law. Also, as discussed next, consider if a client asks you to take action that goes beyond the limits of the law. Lawyers should understand any ethical and moral issues that may arise when problem solving.

C. Recognize Ethical and Moral Issues

In addition to understanding the relevant law and how it could apply to your client's problem, consider possible ethical and moral issues that may arise when developing options to solve your client's problem. Like researching legal sources, such as cases and statutes, you need to research ethical rules in your jurisdiction. Understanding the ethical rules applicable to lawyers is necessary to identify and resolve potential ethical issues when solving your client's problem.

In law school, you probably read about ethical dilemmas in a casebook or hypothetical, while focusing on the rules of professional responsibility in the abstract; however, the ethical and moral dilemmas may be murkier in practice. Life is messy, and

> **STAGES OF PROBLEM SOLVING**
>
> - Identify the problem
>   - Identify the client
>   - Determine the facts
> - **Develop options**
>   - Identify the client's objectives
>   - Understand the relevant law
>   - **Recognize ethical and moral issues**
>   - Consider creative solutions
>   - Collaborate
> - Evaluate the options
> - Generate and implement a plan
> - Reflect on the solution

clients may have complex lives, difficult relationships, and have ethics, morals, and values that differ from their lawyer. To best serve the clients, lawyers should not impose their own values when giving legal advice or recommending how to proceed to solve a client's problem. When confronted with ethical and moral issues in trying to solve a client's problem, being a mindful lawyer may lead to more ethical behavior as practicing mindfulness involves intentional awareness to ourselves, others, and our environment.

Just because the law may allow a particular course of action to solve a client's problem, it does not mean it is the best solution. Lawyers should consider their own ethics and morals, as well as those of their client. Does the client want to proceed right up to the limits of what the law allows? For example, a client may decide to breach a contract and pay damages rather than comply with the contract. Does the client want to do the right thing even if the law doesn't require it? What if the client wants to apologize but that apology could be admitted in court against the client? What if the client wants to take measures to fix a problem but that may lead to your client being held liable?

Numerous ethical issues may arise when problem solving. Some of the common ethical issues were already mentioned earlier in this book when discussing the importance of identifying your client. While you will learn about ethics in your professional responsibility class in law school, ethical traps may not be so obvious and may be more ambiguous when problem solving in practice. Most states have adopted, in whole or in part, the ABA Model Rules of Professional Conduct; however, you should consult the specific professional conduct rules that apply in your jurisdiction, including possible exceptions, and keep abreast of any changes.

Being aware of some of the common ethical issues may help you avoid them. Violating ethical rules could result in a range of consequences, from losing clients to losing your job, or even losing your law license. Even if action or lack of action may not result in a violation of an ethical rule, if it is contrary to your own morals, it may lead to unhappiness or dissatisfaction. Below are a few common issues you may likely face in practice when problem solving. While there may be exceptions to professional rules that are relevant in these common issues, having a basic understanding of these issues will help you recognize possible ethical and moral concerns when problem solving.

1. *Conflict of Interest*

Do not represent a client if it could conflict with the representation of another.[4] You may unknowingly represent a party adverse to a current client. In addition to understanding who your clients are, recognize who your clients' adversaries are and who your potential clients could be.

Use a conflict-checking system to check for conflicts of interest. Use it at the outset during the client intake process before receiving any confidential information, not after representation has begun. Do not rely on memory for conflict checking. A conflict-checking database should include as much information as possible, such as names and contacts linked to files and cases; the status of that file/case, including whether it is an open or closed case; and the relationship you or your employer had with the contact, adversaries, related contacts, or third-parties.

2. *Formation of a Lawyer-Client Relationship*

Be aware that anyone may be a potential client and you may stumble into a lawyer-client relationship without intending to form such a relationship or having any formal agreement. A person may ask you a legal question that you agree to answer or a person may share information with you that you agree to look into. If you know or reasonably should know that the person is reasonably relying on you to provide legal services, a lawyer-client relationship may arise.[5]

Once a lawyer-client relationship results—even inadvertently—it triggers all the responsibilities and obligations of that lawyer-client relationship, such as loyalty, competency, diligence, and confidentiality.[6] To avoid inadvertent formation of a lawyer-client relationship, be aware of the possible formation of that relationship and be explicit about whether you are representing the person.

3. *Acting at the Direction of a Supervisor*

Lawyers should not assume that "my boss made me do it" will excuse them from their professional obligations. You are still bound by the rules of professional responsibility.[7] Even if a subordinate lawyer refuses to comply with a supervisor's unethical directives, you may have to report the unethical direction of your supervisor to a professional authority.[8]

Remember how much time, energy, and effort it takes to obtain a law degree and law license. Also, be mindful of why you decided to become a lawyer. Don't jeopardize your ability to practice law, help clients, and enjoy job satisfaction and happiness by neglecting to consider the ethical and moral concerns that may arise when problem solving.

D. Consider Creative Solutions

If you were asked to give examples of creative people, would lawyers be on your list? As discussed earlier in the creativity part of this book, lawyers are not just legal technicians, approaching a problem as an intellectual endeavor. Lawyers should consider creative solutions when solving problems.

> **STAGES OF PROBLEM SOLVING**
>
> - Identify the problem
>   - Identify the client
>   - Determine the facts
> - **Develop options**
>   - Identify the client's objectives
>   - Recognize the legal challenges and opportunities
>   - Recognize the ethical and moral concerns
>   - **Consider creative solutions**
>   - Collaborate
> - Evaluate the options
> - Generate and implement a plan
> - Reflect on the solution

Lawyers frequently rush into litigation, pursue some legal solutions, or overcomplicate solutions. When considering creative solutions, review possible nonlegal solutions, including alternative dispute resolution options. Consider whether doing nothing would be a reasonable option worth considering. Think about the simplest solution. Would an apology suffice or would it create more problems? Does the client want monetary compensation? Remember problems involve real people. Look at the problem from different perspectives and interests—your opponent's perspective, a judge's perspective, and any other interested persons' perspectives.

Keep in mind the kinds of creative thinking legal employers want and clients need, and how creativity is connected to problem solving. Don't let your fear of making a mistake inhibit your creative thinking. To be creative, take away the urge to evaluate ideas at the same time you are generating ideas. Work on your creativity muscle like you do when you focus on learning the law. What have you have done in your law school courses to foster or promote creative thinking? What could you do differently?

In earlier parts of the book you learned how mindfulness reduces stress and anxiety, leading to an open and curious space to creatively process information in a nonjudgmental and nonbiased way. Refer back to the creativity part of this book, as it will remind you of what it means to be creative and of strategies you can use to maximize your creative potential.

When developing possible solutions to a client's problem, think outside the legal box. Better yet, think as if there is no box. Try to see connections between things that may not seem to be related. For example, have you ever played the game *Apples to Apples*?

E. Collaborate

Collaborating when problem solving can often lead to a better solution than any you could have developed if you worked alone.

While law students often work in isolation, in practice, lawyers' ability to work with other lawyers and form relationships is critical to succeed. Collaboration allows lawyers and clients to get the most benefit from the differences and strengths among team members. Group collaboration with prepared teammates with diverse experiences and backgrounds can generate helpful options. Collaboration involves shared decision making and shared responsibility for an outcome to a problem, including giving and receiving feedback.

STAGES OF PROBLEM SOLVING

- Identify the problem
  - Identify the client
  - Determine the facts
- **Develop options**
  - Identify the client's objectives
  - Understand the relevant law
  - Recognize ethical and moral issues
  - Consider creative solutions
  - **Collaborate**
- Evaluate the options
- Generate and implement a plan
- Reflect on the solution

Working with others does not necessarily mean collaboration is achieved. For example, in an input model, a hierarchal system is in place where one person at the top makes decisions after discussions with others.[9]

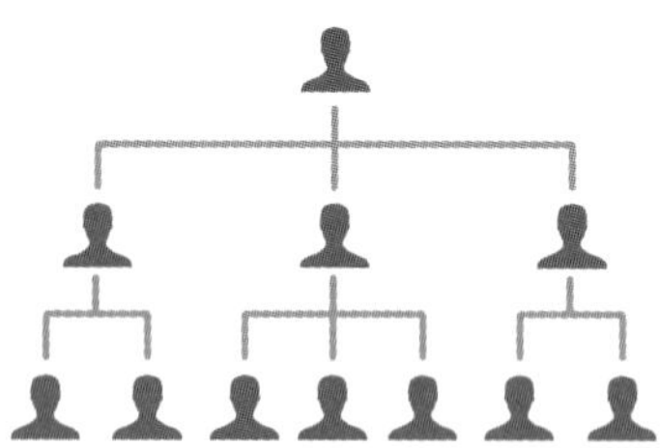

Input Model

In contrast, in a parallel model, tasks are delegated, and team members work independently and separately on tasks and don't share decision making or exchange ideas.[10]

Parallel Model

Seeking input from people with different perspectives, diverse backgrounds, and different experiences, while listening and learning about their interests and positions, can help you see a problem in different ways and foster creative solutions. As noted earlier in this book, cultural competence requires the ability to see problems through the eyes of another. This plays an important role in successful collaboration. Acknowledging and appreciating each person's input and being amenable to incorporating others' ideas can help a group working together to reach a consensus.

When collaborating, also keep the focus on the interests rather than positions of your client or teammates you are collaborating with to solve the problem. As defined earlier in the book regarding identifying your client's objectives, a person's position is the outcome she says she wants. A person's interest is the reason why she wants that outcome. Avoid making any assumptions regarding interests and positions. If you are unsure of a person's position and interest, ask questions to confirm your understanding. Be sensitive to others' nonlegal concerns when working towards a solution.

STAGES OF TEAM DEVELOPMENT

- Forming
- Storming
- Norming
- Performing

In working with others to achieve the best solution for a client, you may go through the common stages of team development: forming, storming, norming, and performing.[11] In the forming stage, colleagues are just getting to know each other. In the storming stage, conflicting views and disagreements develop. In the norming stage, teammates begin to work more efficiently. Finally, in the performing stage, colleagues have incorporated the strengths of each colleague and are operating most effectively. Teamwork is a skill that can be critical to successfully solving a client's problem. Consider how you collaborate, including how your team members communicate, complete the work, make decisions, and cooperate with each other. Understanding the importance of collaboration, focusing on interests as opposed to positions, and appreciating the stages of team development, can help you navigate group dynamics and maximize collaboration to solve a client's problems.

F. Develop Options Checklists

1. Identify the Client's Objectives Checklist

- ❑ What is the client's position?
- ❑ What is the client's interest?
- ❑ What is the client's objective(s)?
    - ❍ Short-term?
    - ❍ Long-term?
    - ❍ Economic?
    - ❍ Emotional?
    - ❍ Personal?

- ❍ Moral?
- ❍ Religious?
- ❍ Political?
- ❍ Psychological?
- ❍ Legal?

- ❑ Is the client's objective SMART?
  - ❍ Specific?
  - ❍ Measurable?
  - ❍ Attainable?
  - ❍ Relevant?
  - ❍ Timely?
- ❑ If the client has more than one objective, are they consistent?
- ❑ If there is more than one objective, what are the priorities?
- ❑ What is the client's best-case scenario and worst case scenario?
- ❑ How risk averse is your client?

2. Understand the Relevant Law and How It Could Apply Checklist

- ❑ Have you researched the relevant law?
- ❑ Have you synthesized the law and reconciled any conflicting authority?
- ❑ What does the law allow?
- ❑ What does the law restrict?
- ❑ Are there exceptions?
- ❑ Is it a case of first impression?
- ❑ Is the law binding or persuasive authority?
- ❑ Has the law been broadly or narrowly construed?
- ❑ Is precedent favorable or unfavorable in cases with similar facts?
- ❑ Are you looking to extend the law?
- ❑ Have you employed the different modes of legal reasoning?

- ❍ inductive/analogical reasoning
- ❍ deductive/rule-based reasoning
- ❍ policy-based reasoning
- ❍ narrative reasoning

- ❑ Is a legal solution the best one to meet the client's objectives?
- ❑ How much time and cost is involved in pursuing legal options?

3. *Recognize the Ethical and Moral Issues Checklist*

- ❑ Have you determined your client's ethical and moral concerns?
- ❑ What are the relevant ethical rules or sources of ethical standards in your jurisdiction?
- ❑ Have you considered whether there are any ethical issues, such as:
  - ❍ Conflict of interest?
  - ❍ Formation of a lawyer-client relationship?
  - ❍ Acting at the direction of a supervisor?
- ❑ Do your own ethics, morals, or values conflict with the client's?
- ❑ Did your own ethics, morals, or values influence how you view the problem and possible solutions?
- ❑ Have you considered whether proposed solutions are ethical?

4. *Consider Creative Solutions Checklist*

- ❑ Have you considered nonlegal solutions?
- ❑ What if the client takes no action, i.e., does nothing?
- ❑ What is the simplest solution?
- ❑ Have you brainstormed all the possible creative solutions without judging them at the outset?

5. *Collaborate Checklist*

- ❑ Have you worked with others on this problem?
- ❑ What perspective does each member of your team bring to working on a solution to a client's problem?

- ❑ Has everyone had an opportunity to voice her input and have diverse views been heard?
- ❑ Did your team go through the different stages of forming, storming, norming, and performing?
  - ❍ How?
  - ❍ What are some examples from each stage?

Chapter Ten

Evaluate the Options

An earlier part of this book discussed Bloom's Taxonomy and identified evaluation and the generation of a solution to a problem as the highest order of thinking. Also, you learned in the creativity part of this book that you don't want to evaluate options at the same time as you are thinking creatively to generate possible solutions. Rather, Verification is the final stage of the creative process when the creator evaluates whether an idea is a good one. Thus, mindfulness and creativity play a role in the next stage of problem solving: evaluating the options.

After identifying a client's problem and developing possible options to solve the problem, you must carefully evaluate the options. When evaluating the options, a lawyer needs to educate her client about the possible outcomes; the likelihood of success of each option; and the costs, risks, and time involved. While a lawyer can review the means and the options to an end, it is the client's decision regarding which option to choose and how to proceed.

A. Choices

When evaluating and weighing options, a lawyer must balance numerous considerations. The first and foremost concern should be whether the solution is consistent with the client's objectives and how risk averse the client is. The short-term and long-term objectives of the client should be reviewed as well. Cost and efficiency are important, too. Other factors to consider include what would be best for the client emotionally, personally, morally, religiously, politically, and psychologically. In addition, it is critical that you examine whether an option would create new problems or make the problem worse.

When evaluating options, you need to predict likely outcomes and determine which one would best fit the client's goals. You may want to use a decision tree to evaluate how to proceed to achieve the client's objectives. Lawyers need to confront uncertainties and inform clients of them. This inherent uncertainty could lead to creative solutions. A decision tree can help a lawyer visualize the best option by considering the cost and benefit analysis and the likelihood of success of different options.

STAGES OF PROBLEM SOLVING

- Identify the problem
  - Identify the client
  - Determine the facts
- Develop options
  - Identify the client's objectives
  - Recognize the legal challenges and opportunities
  - Understand the ethical and moral concerns
  - Consider creative solutions
  - Collaborate
- **Evaluate the options**
- Generate and implement a plan
- Reflect on the solution

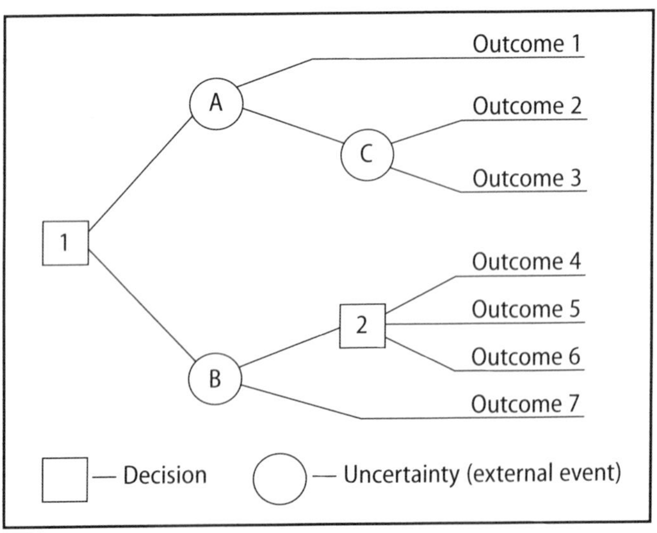

Decision Tree Model

A decision tree shows possible outcomes in a concrete, visual display for a lawyer and her client, and helps the lawyer be thorough. Using a graph or visual map that looks like a tree or flowchart, insert your proposed solutions and then their possible consequences, both good/best case and bad/worst case scenarios; risks; costs; and estimated time to solve the client's problem. Include legal and nonlegal solutions and procedural options.

Below is an example of a decision tree for the options of settling a case or going to trial. Consider what the most certain outcome is. Determine which outcome may be the costliest. How much time would a trial take versus a settlement? Would a settlement be public? Would the trial be public? While settling may be the most certain and final option, if your client is not risk averse, then going to trial, even with an uncertain outcome, may align more with your client's objectives.

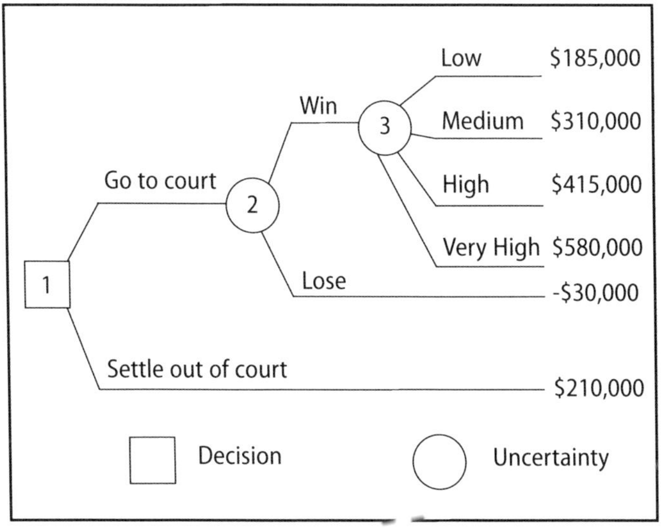

Decision Tree
Possible Outcomes of Decision to Settle or Go to Court

B. Evaluate the Options Checklist

- ❑ Are the proposed solutions consistent with the client's goals?
- ❑ What would happen if you did nothing?
- ❑ What could make the problem worse?
- ❑ How can you avoid a problem?
- ❑ How risk averse is your client?
- ❑ Have you utilized a decision tree to review possible options?

Chapter Eleven

Generate and Implement a Plan

After identifying the client's problem and developing and evaluating options, the next stage is to generate and implement a plan to solve the client's problem. Whether pursuing a theory of litigation, a deal, or a conflict resolution strategy, empower the client to make the ultimate decision of how to proceed. Lawyers are called "counsel" or "counselors" for a reason.

A. What's the Plan?

Develop a plan of action, determine next steps, and implement them. Continue to be receptive to new ideas or adjustments along the way if new information arises. Finally, give the client an opportunity to ask questions.

Make sure to be clear regarding concrete steps, including clarifying the responsibilities of the lawyer and the client. The client needs to understand whether the lawyer or client is taking action, what that action is, and how it will be achieved. Also, be explicit about deadlines.

When generating a plan and proceeding to implement it to solve a client's problem, make sure you have aligned the solution with achieving the client's objectives. In deciding whether the lawyer, as opposed to the client, should proceed with certain tasks, consider costs, efficiency, and whether it would help or hurt the problem.

STAGES OF PROBLEM SOLVING

- Identify the problem
    - Identify the client
    - Determine the facts
- Develop options
    - Identify the client's objectives
    - Recognize the legal challenges and opportunities
    - Understand the ethical and moral concerns
    - Consider creative solutions
    - Collaborate
- Evaluate the options
- **Generate and implement a plan**
- Reflect on the solution

B. Generate and Implement a Plan Checklist

- ❑ Have you set out the concrete and specific steps/plan of action?
- ❑ Have you determined whether the lawyer, client, or another will be doing each step listed above?
- ❑ When will each step in the plan occur?
- ❑ Why have you decided on this plan and the steps in it?
- ❑ How will the tasks be done (via phone call, email, letter, memo, meeting, etc.)?

Chapter Twelve

Reflect on the Solution

You may be tempted to skip this next stage of the problem-solving process, thinking you are too busy to reflect. But wait. In addition to setting your intention in a mindful way at the outset, reflection is critical to future success. While problem solving, reflect on your approaches and steps taken.[1] Reflect at the conclusion of the problem-solving process as well. Reflection can help reduce errors or missteps in the future and increase resiliency.

A. Looking Back and Moving Forward

Problem solving involves reflection and deliberative practice. Reflection is one way to develop and increase overall awareness, professional judgment, cultural competency, and professional identity. While in law school, you may have focused mainly on learning the law and legal theories as well as their application to facts, but knowledge of the law is not enough. The mindfulness part of this book shows that knowledge is at the bottom of the Bloom's Taxonomy pyramid. Evaluation and the creation of a solution to a problem are at the top. Metacognitive learning, thinking about how you learn, and reflective learning, thinking about why and why not, will make you a better problem solver.

Effective problem solving should involve reflection for the best results in future problems. As discussed earlier in this book, what is important is not whether you made a mistake, but whether you mindfully use grit and resiliency to learn from that mistake.

Also, the creativity part of this book provided helpful examples of the role of failures in the creative process. A trip to the Museum

of Failure shows that. It also illustrated how many creative people persevered in the face of failure. Numerous other "famous failures" come to mind: Michael Jordan, Walt Disney, and Oprah Winfrey, just to name a few. They learned from their mistakes and setbacks and went on to become highly successful. You can, too!

STAGES OF PROBLEM SOLVING

- Identify the problem
  - Identify the client
  - Determine the facts
- Develop options
  - Identify the client's objectives
  - Recognize the legal challenges and opportunities
  - Understand the ethical and moral concerns
  - Consider creative solutions
  - Collaborate
- Evaluate the options
- Generate and implement a plan
- **Reflect on the solution**

Think about what you learned from your mistakes in the different stages of problem solving and how that reflection can make you a better problem solver in the future. You sometimes learn more from your mistakes than your successes. By reflecting on your problem-solving experiences, you can transfer lessons learned to solve different types of legal problems for different clients in virtually any practice area. You are on your way to becoming a mindful and creative problem solver!

B. Reflect on the Solution Checklist

- ❑ Did you practice mindfulness during the problem-solving process?
- ❑ Was the approach to solving the client's problem effective?
- ❑ Did the solution achieve the client's objectives?
- ❑ Did you reflect contemporaneously during the problem-solving process?
- ❑ Were redirection and adjustments needed and if so, what did you do to adapt your approach?
- ❑ At what points in the problem-solving process did you make choices?
- ❑ Why did you make those choices?
- ❑ Did your personal preferences, biases, experiences, and characteristics influence your decisions?
- ❑ Did your perception of others' preferences, biases, experiences, and characteristics affect you when solving the problem?
- ❑ Were there any societal, economic, political, or other external pressures that influenced how you solved the problem?
- ❑ What would you do differently the next time you face a similar problem?

Part V

Appendices

Earlier in this book, you read explanations, illustrations, and checklists for being a mindful and creative problem solver. This part of the book helps you assess and apply what you have learned. Appendix One contains a capstone exercise that synthesizes the material discussed earlier in the book in the form of a problem you are asked to consider how you would solve. In addition, a comprehensive set of checklists in Appendix Two incorporates the checklists that were provided throughout the book. Finally, Appendix Three provides a list of additional resources that you can consult to continue your journey to become a mindful and creative problem solver.

Appendix One

Capstone Exercise

Read through the problem below, keeping in mind what you have previously read in this book. You may find it helpful to make notes in the margin as you read through the client's problem. Use the checklists in the next Appendix to prepare to mindfully and creatively consider how you might solve the problem.

You rush out the door, late, coffee in hand, running to catch the train to work. You know there is a new client meeting that morning the senior partner wanted you to attend. It is an interesting case involving a high school student who was suspended from school for violating her school's dress code policy. You find yourself starting to get a headache as you think over the case on your commute in. You want to be sharp for the meeting and you know this particular partner will want you to take good notes and also to ask good questions.

You start to review the client's file while you try to answer the dozen emails that have flooded your inbox since you boarded the train. Allison Wright is a senior in high school and is the daughter of your parents' friend. Allison is an honors student and talented soccer player who has a scholarship to a prestigious university contingent upon her successful graduation. Allison was disciplined once during her junior year when she was chanting loudly in support of a presidential candidate during a school assembly. Allison is very involved in politics and is known to be passionate about social issues and causes. One of Allison's best friends is a Muslim student, Mina Ahmed, who moved to town when the girls were in 8th grade. Mina plays soccer as well. The girls have spent a lot of time at each other's homes over the years. Mina's family attends a local mosque regularly, and Allison has accompanied them multiple times as she is very interested in learning about other religions. Allison's family is Baptist.

You try to balance your coffee, phone, and case file as the train abruptly screeches to a stop at the next station. Your coffee spills on the file. You pull out a muffin to eat and you notice you have a voice mail which you listen to. It is from the partner who tells you she is running late and you will need to meet with the client yourself. You think back to your last client interview and your stomach tenses up.

The commuters' conversation around you grows louder, so you put in your earbuds and listen to some music as you continue to read Allison's case file. You see from the file that as the anniversary of 9/11 approached and anti-Muslim rhetoric was increasing during the presidential campaign, Mina decided to recommit to her religion by wearing a headscarf. She confided in Allison that she was nervous to wear the headscarf to school, because their school is not very diverse and there are no other Muslim students wearing headscarves to school. Mina was repeatedly questioned about wearing the headscarf and even called a terrorist the first day she wore it. She confided again to Allison that she felt very isolated and alone in her religious practice, but felt even more compelled to practice this tenet of her religion given the reaction she received.

You notice you are starting to sweat as the train is full and you are cramped next to another commuter sitting next to you. You realize you are almost at your stop. You make a note in your phone to remember to pick up your dry cleaning at lunch. You need that navy-blue suit for a deposition tomorrow, so you cannot forget. You flip through the notes in the file to finish reviewing it before arriving at work.

You read that Allison decided to support her friend by also wearing a headscarf to school. The school has a dress code which prohibits "the wearing of any head covering" while on school campus. The first day Allison wore the headscarf to school, she was teased and called a "towel head" and a terrorist. Allison told people that she was supporting her friend Mina and her right to practice one of the world's great religions. At the end of the day, Allison was called to the principal's office and told that she was in violation of the school dress code and that she would have to remove the headscarf in order to attend school. When Allison wore the headscarf again the next day, she was suspended.

Allison and her parents appealed to the school board, who reaffirmed her suspension. Allison and her parents are meeting with your law firm to discuss and evaluate their options.

Appendix Two

Checklists

Use the following checklists to first reflect on how you might already be a mindful and creative problem solver. Engaging in this self-reflection may help you realize you already bring important assets to the legal table. Then, apply the checklists to guide you to be a mindful and creative problem solver.

Checklist A. Mindfulness Training

- ❑ How have you typically studied in the past?
  - ❍ Where?
  - ❍ For how long?
  - ❍ Do you sometimes become distracted? By what?
- ❑ Consider a time when you were under stress. How did it affect you physically? Mentally?
- ❑ Consider how you have dealt with stress in the past. Were you successful? What challenges have you found are created by stress?
- ❑ Can you think of a time where you handled stress well? What did you do? How did you do that?

Checklist B. Train Your Brain

Reflect on a recent study or work session. What was your intention before you began? Were you distracted? Was your physical space conducive to the work you were trying to accomplish? Once you have tried the techniques described in this book, use this checklist to evaluate your work:

- ❑ Did you create a plan before you began?
- ❑ Did you clear your physical space to make it conducive and specific to the work at hand?
- ❑ Did you clear your mental space to help eliminate distractions and create a focused learning environment?
- ❑ Did you note items distracting you so that you could attend to them later?
- ❑ Did you try to work with grit and resiliency, reminding yourself not to dwell on past mistakes or failures?

Checklist C. Creativity 101

- ❑ Consider the creativity myths that you read about.
  - ❍ Before you read about them, did you believe any of them?
    - Did you believe that smarter people are more creative?
    - Did you believe that creativity only applies to the arts?
    - Did you believe that creativity is limited to only a rare few special people?
    - Did you believe that creativity can't be controlled and that you just need to sit around and wait for inspiration to strike?
    - Did you believe that creativity can't be fostered or taught?
    - Did you believe that people are creative in isolation and that creativity is not a collaborative process?
  - ❍ If so, have you been able to dispel the myth(s) so that it (they) can no longer serve as a barrier to your creative potential?
- ❑ Are you surprised that creativity can be measured? Why or why not?
- ❑ Do you consider yourself a convergent thinker or a divergent thinker? Both? Explain.
- ❑ Measure your creativity—
  - ❍ In three minutes, draw as many drawings as you can out of the rectangles below. After three minutes, review your responses. Are they original, fluent, flexible, and elaborate?

- ❍ Now, take three minutes and list as many possible uses of a brick as you can. How did you do?

❑ Can you think of an example of a creative idea that you came up with to solve an everyday problem?

Checklist D. Creativity: Why It's Needed Now More Than Ever

- ❑ Before you read this book, did you think that it was important to be creative? Why or why not?
    - ❍ Has your opinion changed? If yes, how has it changed? If no, why not?
- ❑ Can you think of other examples that exemplify the unprecedented rate of change in society today?
- ❑ Did it surprise you that 1,500 CEOs from 50 countries identified creativity as the most important leadership competency? Why or why not?
- ❑ Can you think of an example of creative lawyering?
- ❑ Did it surprise you that creativity is declining in the United States? Why or why not?
- ❑ Reflect on the speculated causes of the decline in creativity scores in the United States. Looking back at your own upbringing and past schooling, do you relate to any of the speculated causes? Do you think these things may have impacted your creativity? For example:
    - ❍ Did your teachers "teach to the test"?
    - ❍ Did your teachers use multiple-choice questions to assess your performance?

Checklist E. Maximizing Your Creative Potential

- ❑ If you answered the question "Are you creative?" in the negative, reflect on why you responded this way. Think about ways you can work towards changing your attitude.
- ❑ Think about a time that you took a risk and it didn't work out the way you wanted it to. What happened? How did you deal with it?
- ❑ Can you think of a time where you struggled with a task or problem? Did you give up? If so, think about why you gave up and how to improve your grit.
- ❑ Think back to the exercises in the book about how to think creatively. How did you do? Did you find that you:
    - ❍ Assumed one right answer?
    - ❍ Made assumptions that were not stated?
    - ❍ Were confused and unsettled by any ambiguities?

The book provided strategies for maximizing your creative potential. The next time you are asked to solve a problem, use the following checklist to evaluate how well you have been able to flex your creative muscle.

- ❑ Did you have the requisite domain knowledge? If not, what did you do to attain it?
- ❑ Did you have a creative attitude? Did you believe that you could generate creative solutions to the problem?
- ❑ Were you willing to take risks or did the fear of failure become an obstacle to generating novel solutions?
- ❑ Did you give up quickly or did you persevere, embracing failures as a first attempt at learning?
- ❑ Did you take a break to allow your mind to unconsciously work on the problem?

- ❏ Did you stop with the first solution that you generated, or did you continue to generate additional "right answers"?
- ❏ While working to solve the problem, did you stop to identify any assumptions that you may have been making? Did you challenge those assumptions, where appropriate?
- ❏ When faced with uncertainty, did you embrace ambiguity and seek to see the problem from different perspectives?

Checklist F. Stages of Problem Solving

- ❑ What are the stages of problem solving?
- ❑ Before beginning to work on solving your client's problem, have you taken the time to set your intention?
- ❑ Have you cleared your physical space to eliminate distractions and maintain your focus on problem solving?

Checklist G. Identify the Client

- ❑ Who is the client?
  - ❍ Is it an individual, government entity, or a corporation?
  - ❍ Is there more than one?
- ❑ Has an attorney-client relationship been formed?
- ❑ What do you know about your client (education, work, family, age, health, prior legal experience, life experience, risk tolerance, resources, time)?

Checklist H. Determine the Facts

❑ What facts do you know?

- ❍ Who?
    - Who are the interested parties?
    - Who are the witnesses?
    - Who have you talked to about the facts?
- ❍ What happened?
- ❍ When?
- ❍ Where?
- ❍ Why?
- ❍ How?

❑ From what source do the facts come from?

- ❍ Have you evaluated the reliability and significance of the information?
- ❍ What possible motivation, agenda, or perspective do the client, witness, parties, or others have in describing the facts?
- ❍ Are you making any assumptions, inferences, or opinions?

❑ What facts do you not know yet?

- ❍ How will you find them out or gather missing facts?

❑ Have you used a combination of open and closed questions to uncover facts?

❑ Have you established a rapport with your client? How?

❑ Have you engaged in active listening?

❑ Have you considered cultural issues, implicit bias, diversity, and inclusion issues that may affect the facts or how the law applies to those facts?

Checklist I. Identify the Client's Objectives

- ❑ What is the client's position?
- ❑ What is the client's interest?
- ❑ What is the client's objective(s)?
    - ❍ Short-term?
    - ❍ Long-term?
    - ❍ Economic?
    - ❍ Emotional?
    - ❍ Personal?
    - ❍ Moral?
    - ❍ Religious?
    - ❍ Political?
    - ❍ Psychological?
    - ❍ Legal?
- ❑ Is the client's objective SMART?
    - ❍ Specific?
    - ❍ Measurable?
    - ❍ Attainable?
    - ❍ Relevant?
    - ❍ Timely?
- ❑ If the client has more than one objective, are they consistent?
- ❑ If there is more than one objective, what are the priorities?
- ❑ What is the client's best-case scenario and worst case scenario?
- ❑ How risk averse is your client?

Checklist J. Understand the Relevant Law and How It Could Apply

- [ ] Have you researched the relevant law?
- [ ] Have you synthesized the law and reconciled any conflicting authority?
- [ ] What does the law allow?
- [ ] What does the law restrict?
- [ ] Are there exceptions?
- [ ] Is it a case of first impression?
- [ ] Is the law binding or persuasive authority?
- [ ] Has the law been broadly or narrowly construed?
- [ ] Is precedent favorable or unfavorable in cases with similar facts?
- [ ] Are you looking to extend the law?
- [ ] Have you employed the different modes of legal reasoning?
    - ❍ inductive/analogical reasoning
    - ❍ deductive/rule-based reasoning
    - ❍ policy-based reasoning
    - ❍ narrative reasoning
- [ ] Is a legal solution the best one to meet the client's objectives?
- [ ] How much time and cost is involved in pursuing legal options?

Checklist K. Recognize the Ethical and Moral Issues

- ❑ Have you determined your client's ethical and moral concerns?
- ❑ What are the relevant ethical rules or sources of ethical standards in your jurisdiction?
- ❑ Have you considered whether there are any ethical issues, such as:
  - ❍ Conflict of interest?
  - ❍ Formation of a lawyer-client relationship?
  - ❍ Acting at the direction of a supervisor?
- ❑ Do your own ethics, morals, or values conflict with the client's?
- ❑ Did your own ethics, morals, or values influence how you view the problem and possible solutions?
- ❑ Have you considered whether proposed solutions are ethical?

Checklist L. Consider Creative Solutions

- ❑ Have you considered nonlegal solutions?
- ❑ What if the client takes no action, i.e., does nothing?
- ❑ What is the simplest solution?
- ❑ Have you brainstormed all the possible creative solutions without judging them at the outset?

Checklist M. Collaborate

- ❑ Have you worked with others on this problem?
- ❑ What perspective does each member of your team bring to working on a solution to a client's problem?
- ❑ Has everyone had an opportunity to voice her input and have diverse views been heard?
- ❑ Did your team go through the different stages of forming, storming, norming, and performing?
    - ❍ How?
    - ❍ What are some examples from each stage?

Checklist N. Evaluate the Options

- ❏ Are the proposed solutions consistent with the client's goals?
- ❏ What would happen if you did nothing?
- ❏ What could make the problem worse?
- ❏ How can you avoid a problem?
- ❏ How risk averse is your client?
- ❏ Have you utilized a decision tree to review possible options?

Checklist O. Generate and Implement a Plan

- ❑ Have you set out the concrete and specific steps/plan of action?
- ❑ Have you determined whether the lawyer, client, or another will be doing each step listed above?
- ❑ When will each step in the plan occur?
- ❑ Why have you decided on this plan and the steps in it?
- ❑ How will the tasks be done (via phone call, email, letter, memo, meeting, etc.)?

Checklist P. Reflect on the Solution

❑ Did you practice mindfulness during the problem-solving process?

❑ Was the approach to solving the client's problem effective?

❑ Did the solution achieve the client's objectives?

❑ Did you reflect contemporaneously during the problem-solving process?

❑ Were redirection and adjustments needed and if so, what did you do to adapt your approach?

❑ At what points in the problem-solving process did you make choices?

❑ Why did you make those choices?

❑ Did your personal preferences, biases, experiences, and characteristics influence your decisions?

❑ Did your perception of others' preferences, biases, experiences, and characteristics affect you when solving the problem?

❑ Were there any societal, economic, political, or other external pressures that influenced how you solved the problem?

❑ What would you do differently the next time you face a similar problem?

Appendix Three

Additional Resources

A. Mindfulness

Sam Anderson, *In Defense of Distraction*, N.Y. Mag., May 17, 2009.

Hillary Burgess, *Deepening the Discourse Using the Legal Mind's Eye: Lessons from Neuroscience and Psychology that Optimize Law School Learning*, 29 Quinnipiac L. Rev. 1 (2011).

Nicholas Carr, The Shallows: What the Internet is Doing to Our Brains (2010).

Angela Duckworth, Grit (2016).

Carol Dweck, Mindset: The New Psychology of Success (2006).

Shailini J. George, *Teaching the Smartphone Generation: How Cognitive Science Can Improve Learning in Law School,* 66 Me. L. Rev. 163 (2013).

Shailini J. George, *The Cure for the Distracted Mind: Why Law Schools Should Teach Mindfulness*, 53 Duq. L. Rev. 216 (2015).

Edward Hallowell, M.D., Driven to Distraction at Work (2015).

J. Patton Hyman, *The Mindful Lawyer: Mindfulness Meditation and Law Practice*, 33 Vt. B.J. 40 (2007).

M.H. Sam Jacobson, *Paying Attention or Fatally Distracted? Concentration, Memory, and Multi-Tasking in a Multi-Media World*, 16 Legal Writing 419 (2010).

Amishi P. Jha et al. *Examining the Protective Effects of Mindfulness Training on Working Memory Capacity and Affective Experience*, 10 Emotion 54 (2010).

Daniel Kahneman, Thinking, Fast and Slow (2011).

Ellen J. Langer, The Power of Mindful Learning (1997).

Rhonda V. Magee, *Educating Lawyers to Meditate?*, 79 U. Mo.-Kan. City L. Rev. 535 (2011).

Michelle D. Miller, *What College Teachers Should Know About Memory: A Perspective from Cognitive Psychology*, 59 C. Teaching 117 (2011).

Annie Murphy Paul, *Your Head Is in the Cloud*, Time, Mar. 12, 2012.

Scott Rogers, *Making a Case for Mindfulness and Law Student Wellness*, ABA (Apr. 13, 2016), http://abaforlawstudents.com/2016/04/13/making-a-case-for-mindfulness-and-law-student-wellness/.

Scott L. Rogers, Mindfulness for Law Students (2009).

Scott Rogers, *Stop, Look, and Listen—Regain Your Focus Through Mindfulness*, 15 A.B.A.: Young L. (2011).

Scott L. Rogers, The Six Minute Solution (2009).

Michael Hunter Schwartz, *Teaching Law by Design: How Learning Theory and Instructional Design Can Inform and Reform Law Teaching*, 38 San Diego L. Rev. 347 (2001).

Daniel J. Siegel, Mindsight: The New Science of Personal Transformation (2010).

Susan L. Smalley, PhD & Diana Winston, Fully Present (2010).

B. Creativity

ABA, Section of Legal Education and Admission to the Bar, Legal Education and Professional Development, *An Education Continuum, Report of the Task Force on Law Schools and the Profession: Narrowing the Gap* (July 1992).

Stephen Bowkett, 100+ Ideas for Teaching Creativity (2007).

Jacob Bronowski, A Sense of Future: Essays in Natural Philosophy (Piero E. Ariotti & Rita Bronoswski eds. 1977).

Po Bronson & Ashley Merryman, *The Creativity Crisis*, NEWSWEEK (July 10, 2010), http://www.newsweek.com/creativity-crisis-74665.

THE CAMBRIDGE HANDBOOK OF CREATIVITY (James C. Kaufman & Robert J. Sternberg eds., 2010).

ARTHUR CROPLEY & DAVID CROPLEY, FOSTERING CREATIVITY (2009).

MIHALEY CSIKSZENTMIHALYI, CREATIVITY: FLOW AND THE PSYCHOLOGY OF DISCOVERY AND INVENTION (1996).

EUROPEAN UNIVERSITY ASSOCIATION, CREATIVITY IN HIGHER EDUCATION: REPORT ON THE EUA CREATIVITY PROJECT 2006-2007 (2007).

DAVID HENRY FELDMAN, MIHALY CSIKSZENTMIHALY, & HOWARD GARDNER, CHANGING THE WORLD: A FRAMEWORK FOR THE STUDY OF CREATIVITY (1994).

JACK FOSTER, HOW TO GET IDEAS (1996).

HARVARD BUSINESS PRESS, FOSTERING CREATIVITY: EXPERT SOLUTIONS TO EVERYDAY CHALLENGES (2010).

SCOTT G. ISAKSEN, K. BRIAN DORVAL, & DONALD J. TREFFINGER, CREATIVE APPROACHES TO PROBLEM SOLVING: A FRAMEWORK FOR INNOVATION AND CHANGE (2011).

TOM KELLEY & DAVID KELLEY, CREATIVE CONFIDENCE: UNLEASHING THE CREATIVE POTENTIAL WITHIN US ALL (2013).

Kyung Hee Kim, *The Creativity Crisis: The Decrease in Creative Thinking Scores on the Torrance Tests of Creative Thinking*, 23 CREATIVITY RES. J. 285 (2011).

Alan M. Lerner, *Law and Lawyering in the Work Place: Building Better Lawyers by Teaching Students to Exercise Critical Judgment as Creative Problem Solver*, 32 AKRON L. REV. 107 (1999).

Todd I. Lubart, *Models of the Creative Process: Past, Present and Future*, 13 CREATIVITY RES. J. 295 (2001).

Erica L. McWilliam, *Is Creativity Teachable? Conceptualising the Creativity/Pedagogy Relationship in Higher Education*, 30TH HERDSA ANNUAL CONFERENCE: ENHANCING HIGHER EDUCATION, THEORY AND SCHOLARSHIP (July 2007).

Carrie Menkel-Meadow, *Aha? Is Creativity Possible in Legal Problem Solving and Teachable in Legal Education?*, 6 HARV. NEGOT. L. REV. 97 (2001).

CARRIE MENKEL-MEADOW, DISPUTE PROCESSING AND CONFLICT RESOLUTION: THEORY, PRACTICE AND POLICY (2003).

MICHAEL MICHALKO, CREATIVE THINKERING: PUTTING YOUR IMAGINATION TO WORK (2011).

MICHAEL MICHALKO, THINKERTOYS: A HANDBOOK OF CREATIVE-THINKING TECHNIQUES (2d ed. 2006).

MICHAEL MICHALKO, THINKPAK: A BRAINSTORMING CARD DECK (2d ed. 2006).

Samantha A. Moppett, *Lawyering Outside the Box: Confronting the Creativity Crisis*, 37 S. ILL. U. L.J. 253 (2013).

Cameron Rhudy, *The Artful Lawyer: Remembering to Use Creative Muscles*, Ms. JD (Oct. 12, 2014), https://ms-jd.org/blog/article/the-artful-lawyer-finding-my-way.

KEN ROBINSON, OUT OF OUR MINDS: LEARNING TO BE CREATIVE (2d ed. 2011).

MARK A. RUNCO, CREATIVITY: THEORIES AND THEMES: RESEARCH, DEVELOPMENT, AND PRACTICE (2007).

R. KEITH SAWYER, EXPLAINING CREATIVITY (2006).

TINA SEELIG, INGENIUS: A CRASH COURSE ON CREATIVITY (2012).

ALANE JORDAN STARKO, CREATIVITY IN THE CLASSROOM (4th ed. 2009), http://www.actedu.in/pdf/creativity.pdf.

Robert Sternberg & Wendy M. Williams, *Teaching for Creativity: Two Dozen Tips*, CTR. FOR DEV. & LEARNING BLOG (Jan. 1, 2003), http://www.cdl.org/articles/teaching-for-creativity-two-dozen-tips/.

Robert D. Strom & Paris S. Strom, *Changing the Rules: Education for Creative Thinking*, 36 J. OF CREATIVE BEHAV. 183 (2002).

ROY STUCKEY ET AL., BEST PRACTICES FOR LEGAL EDUCATION: A VISION AND A ROADMAP (2007).

WILLIAM M. SULLIVAN ET AL., EDUCATING LAWYERS: PREPARATION FOR THE PROFESSION OF LAW (2007).

Matthew Swyers, *5 Steps to Thinking Outside of the Box*, INC. (Feb. 3, 2012), https://www.inc.com/matthew-swyers/5-steps-to-thinking-outside-of-the-box.html.

Steve Tomasco, *IBM 2010 Global CEO Study*, IBM (May 18, 2010), https://www-03.ibm.com/press/us/en/pressrelease/31670.wss.

Roger von Oech, A Whack on the Side of the Head: How You Can Be More Creative (1990).

Janet Weinstein & Linda Morton, *Stuck in a Rut: The Role of Creative Thinking in Problem Solving and Legal Education*, 9 Clinical L. Rev. 835 (2003).

Richard Wiseman, How to Recognize Hidden Opportunities: Did You Spot the Gorilla? (2011).

Robert Yeamans, *Creativity and Legal Education*, 23 J. Legal Educ. 381 (1971).

James Webb Young, A Technique for Producing Ideas (2003).

C. Problem Solving

ABA, *Legal Education, ADR, and Practical Problem Solving Project* (LEAPS), http://leaps.uoregon.edu.

Susan Bryant, *Collaboration in Law Practice: A Satisfying and Productive Process for a Diverse Profession*, 17 Vt. L. Rev. 459 (1993).

Timothy Casey, *Reflective Practice in Legal Education: The Stages of Reflection*, 20 Clinical L. Rev. 317 (2014).

Clark Cunningham, *What Do Clients Want from Their Lawyers?* (Georgia State University College of Law, Legal Studies Research Paper Series, Paper No. 2010, 2009), http://ssrn.com/abstract=1505616.

D. De Gallow, *What is Problem-Based Learning?*, Problem-Based Learning Inst., (Mar. 2013), http://www.pbl.uci.edu/whatispbl.html.

Scott Fruehwald, Think Like a Lawyer 210 (2013).

Larry O. Natt Gantt, *The Pedagogy of Problem Solving: Applying Cognitive Science to Teaching Legal Problem Solving*, 45 Creighton L. Rev. 699 (2012).

Alexandra Hanson Harding, Step-by-Step Guide to Win-Win Negotiating Every Day (2015).

Harvard Law Sch., HARV. L. SCH.: PROBLEM SOLVING WORKSHOP, http://hls.harvard.edu/dept/academics/winter-term/problem-solving-workshop/.

Harvard Law Sch., HARV. L. SCH.: THE CASE STUD., http://casestudies.law.harvard.edu/.

Anne Hewitt, *Give Me a Fish or Teach Me to Fish? Developing Law Students' Capacity for Lifelong Learning* (U. of Adelaide Law Research Paper, Paper No. 2013-01, 2013), http://ssrn.com/abstract=2213645.

Keith H. Hirokawa, *Critical Enculturation: Using Problems to Teach Law*, 2 DREXEL L. REV. 1 (2009).

Steven J. Johansen, *It's Not About the Grades . . . Really*, 21 PERSPECTIVES: TEACHING LEGAL RES. & WRITING 1 (2012).

Tonya Kowalski, *True North: Navigating for the Transfer of Learning in Legal Education*, 34 SEATTLE U. L. REV. 51 (2010).

Katherine R. Kruse, *Biting Off What They Can Chew: Strategies for Involving Students in Problem-Solving Beyond Individual Client Representation*, 8 CLINICAL L. REV. 405 (2002).

LAWMEETS, http://www.lawmeets.com.

Shirley Lung, *The Problem Method: No Simple Solution*, 45 WILLAMETTE L. REV. 723 (2009).

Barbara McAdoo, Sharon Press, & Chelsea Griffin, *It's Time to Get it Right: Problem-Solving in the First-Year Curriculum*, 39 WASH. U. J.L. & POL'Y 39 (2012).

Carrie Menkel-Meadow, *Aha? Is Creativity Possible in Legal Problem Solving and Teachable in Legal Negotiation*, 6 HARV. NEGOT. L. REV. 97 (2001).

Samantha A. Moppett, *Lawyering Outside the Box: Confronting the Creativity Crisis*, 37 S. ILL. U. L.J. 253 (2013).

Linda Morton, *Teaching Creative Problem Solving: A Paradigmatic Approach*, 34 CAL. W.L. REV. 375 (1997-98).

Myron Moskovitz, *Beyond the Case Method: It's Time to Teach with Problems*, 42 J. LEGAL EDUC. 241 (1992).

Stephen Nathanson, *Problem-Solving in Professional Legal Education*, 7 J. PROF. LEGAL EDUC. 121 (1989).

RICHARD K. NEUMANN, JR., TRANSACTIONAL LAWYERING SKILLS: CLIENT INTERVIEWING, COUNSELING, AND NEGOTIATION (2012).

John Palfrey & Lisa Brem, *How to Approach a Case Study in a Problem Solving Workshop*, HARV. L. SCHOOL: THE CASE STUDIES (2012), http://casestudies.law.harvard.edu/how-to-approach-a-case-study-in-a-problem-solving-workshop/.

Todd E. Pettys, *The Analytic Classroom*, 60 BUFF. L. REV. 1255 (2012).

James Rhem, *Problem-Based Learning: An Introduction*, 8 NAT'L TEACHING & LEARNING FORUM 1 (1998).

DAVID ROMANTZ & KATHLEEN ELLIOTT VINSON, LEGAL ANALYSIS: THE FUNDAMENTAL SKILL (2009).

Joseph William Singer, *How Law Professors Can Write a Problem Solving Case*, HARV. L. SCH.: THE CASE STUD. BLOG (Aug. 20, 2013), http://blogs.law.harvard.edu/hlscasestudies/2013/08/20/.

Joseph William Singer, *How to Be a Good Team Member*, HARV. L. SCH.: THE CASE STUD., http://casestudies.law.harvard.edu/joseph-william-singer/.

Joseph William Singer, *Problem Solving for Lawyers*, HARV. L. SCH.: THE CASE STUD., http://casestudies.law.harvard.edu/joseph-william-singer/.

Joseph William Singer & Todd D. Rakoff, *Problem Solving for First-Year Law Students*, 7 ELON L. REV. 413 (2015).

Tracy Thomas, *Teaching Remedies as Problem-Solving: Keeping it Real*, 57 ST. LOUIS U. L.J. 673 (2013).

Bruce W. Tuckman, *Developmental Sequence in Small Groups*, GROUP FACILITATION: A RES. & APPLICATIONS J. (2001), *available at* http://openvce.net/sites/default/files/Tuckman1965DevelopmentalSequence.pdf.

Kathleen Elliott Vinson, *What's Your Problem?*, 44 STETSON L. REV. 777 (2015).

GRANT WIGGINS & JAY MCTIGHT, UNDERSTANDING BY DESIGN (2000).

Endnotes

Chapter Two

1. Issie Lapowsky, *Don't Multitask: Your Brain Will Thank You*, TIME (Apr. 17, 2013), http://business.time.com/2013/04/17/dont-multitask-your-brain-will-thank-you/.

2. Patricia Armstrong, *Bloom's Taxonomy*, VANDERBILT UNIVERSITY, https://cft.vanderbilt.edu/guides-sub-pages/blooms-taxonomy/.

3. *Id.*

4. Sandra Bond Chapman, *Go Full Frontal to Be Smart*, PSYCHOL. TODAY (Jan. 23, 2013), https://www.psychologytoday.com/blog/make-your-brain-smarter/201301/go-full-frontal-be-smart.

5. *Parietal Lobe*, SCIENCEDIRECT, http://www.sciencedirect.com/topics/neuroscience/parietal-lobe.

6. SCOTT L. ROGERS, MINDFULNESS FOR LAW STUDENTS (2009); Amy F. T. Arnsten, *Stress Signaling Pathways*, NCBI, (Jun. 2009), https://www.ncbi.nlm.nih.gov/pmc/articles/PMC2907136/.

7. Jan L. Jacobowitz, *The Benefits of Mindfulness for Litigators*, A.B.A. (2013), https://www.americanbar.org/publications/litigation_journal/2012_13/spring/benefits-mindfulness.html.

8. *History of MBSR*, UMASS MEDICAL SCHOOL, http://www.umassmed.edu/cfm/mindfulness-based-programs/mbsr-courses/about-mbsr/history-of-mbsr/.

Chapter Three

1. Deepak Chopra, *5 Steps to Setting Powerful Intentions*, THE CHOPRA CENTER, http://www.chopra.com/articles/5-steps-to-setting-powerful-intentions#sm.00001d8n15ouoee3kuiv4tu6gmw41.

2. Christine Rosen, *The Myth of Multitasking*, 20 NEW ATLANTIS 105, 106 (2008).

3. *Beginner's Breathing Meditation: Free Relaxation Script*, Inner Health Studio, http://www.innerhealthstudio.com/breathing-meditation.html.

4. Edward M. Hallowell, Driven to Distraction at Work 198 (2015).

5. Angela Duckworth, GRIT: The Power of Passion and Perseverance 8–11 (2016).

6. *Id.* at 42–46. Copyright © 2016 by Angela Duckworth. Reprinted with the permission of Scribner, a division of Simon & Schuster, Inc. All rights reserved.

7. *Id.* at 55–56.

8. Carol Dweck, Mindset: The New Psychology of Success 53–54 (2007).

Chapter Four

1. Arthur Koestler, The Act of Creation 120 (1964).

2. Interview with Steve Jobs, *Business Week* (2004).

3. Peter Nilsson, *Four Ways to Measure Creativity*, Sense and Sensation (Mar. 24, 2012), http://www.senseandsensation.com/2012/03/assessing-creativity.html. Reprinted with permission of author. All rights reserved.

4. Todd Anderson, *Test Your Creativity: 5 Classic Creative Challenges*, 99u, http://99u.com/articles/7160/test-your-creativity-5-classic-creative-challenges.

Chapter Five

1. Steve Tomasco, *IBM 2010 Global CEO Study*, IBM (May 18, 2010), https://www-03.ibm.com/press/us/en/pressrelease/31670.wss.

2. Brief for Petitioner Appellant at 24, *Alaska Dept. of Envtl. Conservation v. U.S. EPA*, 298 F.3d 814 (2001) (No. 02-658), 2003 WL 2010655.

3. Diane F. Baker & Susan J. Baker, *To "Catch the Sparkling Glow": A Canvas for Creativity in the Management Classroom*, 11 Acad. Manag. Learn & Educ. 704–21 (2012).

Chapter Six

1. Michael Michalko, Thinkertoys: A Handbook of Creative-Thinking Techniques 10 (2006).

2. Carol Dweck, Mindset: The New Psychology of Success 53–54 (2007).

3. J.P. Gownder, et al., *How Enterprise Smart Glasses Will Drive Workforce Enablement*, FORRESTER (Apr. 21, 2016), https://www.forrester.com/report/How+Enterprise+Smart+Glasses+Will+Drive+Workforce+Enablement/-/E-RES133722.

4. MICHAEL MICHALKO, CREATIVE THINKERING: PUTTING YOUR IMAGINATION TO WORK 132 (2011).

5. ROGER VON OECH, A WHACK ON THE SIDE OF THE HEAD: HOW YOU CAN BE MORE CREATIVE 22 (1990).

6. 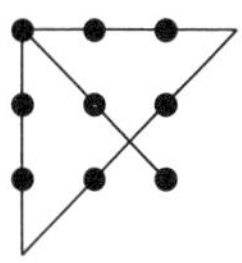

7. MICHAEL MICHALKO, THINKERTOYS: A HANDBOOK OF CREATIVE-THINKING TECHNIQUES 44, 47 (2006).

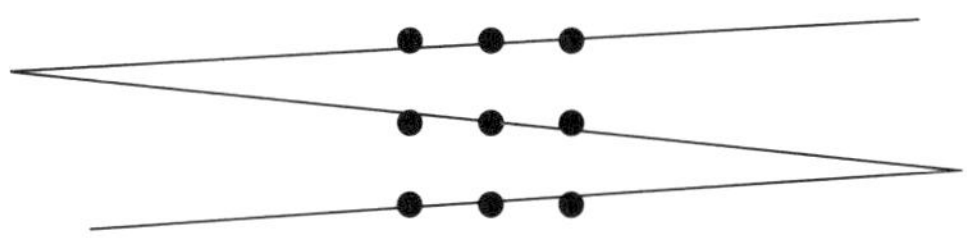

8. *Id.* at 45.

9. Alex J. Hurder, *Negotiating the Lawyer-Client Relationship: A Search for Equality and Collaboration*, 44 BUFF. L. REV. 71, 71–73 (1996); Clark D. Cunningham, *The Lawyer as Translator, Representation as Text: Towards an Ethnography of Legal Discourse*, 77 CORNELL L. REV. 1298 (1992) (referring to lawyers as professors and students as clinic students).

10. RICHARD WISEMAN, DID YOU SPOT THE GORILLA? HOW TO RECOGNISE HIDDEN OPPORTUNITIES 35 (2004).

11. MICHAEL MICHALKO, THINKERTOYS: A HANDBOOK OF CREATIVE-THINKING TECHNIQUES 44–45 (2006).

12. *Id.*

13. Matthew Swyers, *5 Steps to Thinking Outside the Box*, INC. (Feb. 3, 2012), https://www.inc.com/matthew-swyers/5-steps-to-thinking-outside-of-the-box.html.

Part IV

1. Joseph William Singer, *Problem Solving for First-Year Law Students,* 7 ELON L. REV. 413 (2015); Kathleen Elliott Vinson, *What's Your Problem?*, 44 STETSON L. REV. 777 (2015); *Problem Solving Workshop*, HARV. L. SCH. (2017) http://hls.harvard.edu/dept/academics/winter-term/problem-solving-workshop/. The Harvard problem solving methodology involves a series of six question to ask at the outset of considering the problem: (1) who is the client?

(2) what are the facts? (3) what are the client's goals? (4) what are the legal constraints and opportunities? (5) what are the ethical and moral constraints? (6) how do you proceed? *See The Case Development Initiative*, HARV. L. SCH., http://casestudies.law.harvard.edu/the-case-development-initiative/.

Chapter Nine

1. ALEXANDRA HANSON-HARDING, STEP-BY-STEP GUIDE TO WIN-WIN NEGOTIATING EVERY DAY 24–26 (2015).

2. *Id.*

3. PETER F. DRUCKER, THE PRACTICE OF MANAGEMENT (1954); George T. Doran, *There's a S.M.A.R.T. Way to Write Management's Goals and Objectives, Management Review*, AMA FORUM 70 (1981).

4. MODEL RULES OF PROF'L CONDUCT R. 1.7 (1983). Rule 1.7 states: "(a) Except as provided in paragraph (b), a lawyer shall not represent a client if the representation involves a concurrent conflict of interest." *Id.*

5. RESTATEMENT (THIRD) OF LAW GOVERNING LAWYERS § 14.1(a)(b) (2000). While the ABA Rules do not define when a lawyer-client relationship is formed, Restatement (Third) of the Law Governing Lawyers provides guidance. *Id.* Section 14 states:

> A relationship of client and lawyer arises when: (1) a person manifests to a lawyer the person's intent that the lawyer provide legal services for the person; and either (a) the lawyer manifests to the person consent to do so; or (b) the lawyer fails to manifest lack of consent to do so, and the lawyer knows or reasonably should know that the person reasonably relies on the lawyer to provide the services.

Id.

6. MODEL RULES OF PROF'L CONDUCT R. 1.18 (1983). Rule 1.18 states:

> (a) A person who consults with a lawyer about the possibility of forming a client-lawyer relationship with respect to a matter is a prospective client; (b) even when no client-lawyer relationship ensues, a lawyer who has learned information from a prospective client shall not use or reveal that information, except as Rule 1.9 would permit with respect to information of a former client.

Id.

7. MODEL RULES OF PROF'L CONDUCT R. 5.2(a) (1983). Rule 5.2 states: "(a) a lawyer is bound by the Rules of Professional Conduct notwithstanding that the lawyer acted at the direction of another person." *Id.* Rule 5.2(b) states: "A subordinate lawyer does not violate the Rules of Professional Conduct if that lawyer acts in accordance with a supervisory lawyer's reasonable resolution of an arguable question of professional duty." *Id.* at R. 5.2(b).

8. Model Rules of Prof'l Conduct R. 8.3 (1983). Rule 8.3 requires "(a) a lawyer who knows that another lawyer has committed a violation of the Rules of Professional Conduct that raises a substantial question as to that lawyer's honesty, trustworthiness or fitness as a lawyer in other respects, shall inform the appropriate professional authority." *Id.*

9. Susan Bryant, *Collaboration in Law Practice: A Satisfying and Productive Process for a Diverse Profession*, 17 Vt. L. Rev. 459, 492–98 (1993). Discussion of types of joint work also adapted from Anne Goldstein, Professor of Law, New York Law School.

10. *Id.*

11. Joseph William Singer, *How to Be a Good Team Member*, Harv. L. Sch.: The Case Stud., http://blogs.law.harvard.edu/joseph-william-singer/.

Chapter Twelve

1. Timothy Casey, *Reflective Practice in Legal Education: The Stages of Reflection*, 20 Clinical L. Rev. 317, 350 (2014).

Index

I

J

K

L

M

N

O